GOOD HOUSEKEEPING

Electric Casserole Cook Book

GOOD HOUSEKEEPING

Electric Casserole Cook Book

by
Good Housekeeping Institute

Illustrated by Vanessa Luff
and Pat Robson

EBURY PRESS
LONDON

Published by Ebury Press
National Magazine House
72 Broadwick Street
London W1V 2BP

First impression 1978
Second impression 1979

ISBN 0 85223 132 6

Home economist Janet Marsh
Designer Derek Morrison
Colour photography by Melvin Grey

Jacket photograph shows

Front
Vegetable soup with bacon dumplings (page 20), Lamb
noisettes in sherry sauce (page 64)

Back
Farmhouse cake (page 92), Plum upside down pudding
(page 85), Strawberry and apricot jams, Tangy lemon curd
and Seville orange marmalade (page 93)

Filmset and printed in Great Britain by
BAS Printers Limited, Over Wallop, Hampshire
and bound by
Cambridge University Press
Cambridge

Contents

Handy cookery charts

CONVERSION TO METRIC MEASUREMENTS

The metric measures in this book are based on a 25 g unit instead of the ounce (28.35 g). Slight adjustments to this basic conversion standard were necessary in some recipes to achieve satisfactory cooking results.

If you want to convert your own recipes from imperial to metric, we suggest you use the same 25 g unit, and use 600 ml in place of 1 pint, with the British Standard 5-ml and 15-ml spoons replacing the old variable teaspoons and tablespoons. These adaptations will sometimes give a slightly smaller recipe quantity.

Note Sets of British Standard metric measuring spoons are available in the following sizes – 2.5 ml, 5 ml, 10 ml and 15 ml.

When measuring milk it is more convenient to use the exact conversion of 568 ml (1 pint).

For more general reference, the following tables will be helpful.

METRIC CONVERSION SCALE

	LIQUID			SOLID	
Imperial	Exact conversion	Recommended ml	Imperial	Exact conversion	Recommended g
¼ pint	142 ml	150 ml	1 oz	28.35 g	25 g
½ pint	284 ml	300 ml	2 oz	56.7 g	50 g
1 pint	568 ml	600 ml	4 oz	113.4 g	100 g
1 ½ pints	851 ml	900 ml	8 oz	226.8 g	225 g
1 ¾ pints	992 ml	1 litre	12 oz	340.2 g	325 g
			14 oz	397.0 g	400 g
For quantities of 1 ¾ pints and over, litres and fractions of a litre have been used.			16 oz (1 lb)	453.6 g	450 g
			1 kilogram (kg) equals 2.2 lb.		

Note Follow either the metric or the imperial measures in the recipes as they are not interchangeable.

RECIPES MARKED ✤ CAN BE FROZEN

SERVINGS
All recipes give 4 servings unless otherwise stated.

Foreword

Cooking with an electric casserole has all sorts of advantages but there's no doubt it's a new technique to master. If you feel you need a little guidance to get the best from this most versatile addition to your kitchen equipment, the *Good Housekeeping Electric Casserole Cook Book* is the answer.

An introductory chapter gives advice on which model to choose. There is a clear explanation of how an electric casserole works and what you can expect from it. It will save you fuel; it will save you worry. There is practically nothing an electric casserole won't cook, from main dishes to soups, desserts and even a cake. We have indicated those recipes that can be frozen successfully.

The recipes are an eye-opener – tempting and enormously varied – and show that rather than imposing limitations, an electric casserole really will widen your repertoire of exciting meals. The Good Housekeeping Institute experts have enjoyed even more than usual the challenge of devising and testing the 200 or so recipes: we hope you will get as much pleasure out of using them.

GOOD HOUSEKEEPING INSTITUTE

All about electric casseroles

Slow cooking has been used as a method of cooking for hundreds of years – ever since someone thought of hanging a pot over an open fire and leaving the contents to cook 'until done'. Many classic recipes using cheaper often tougher cuts of meat and boiling fowl follow the principle of long slow simmering to tenderise the meat. This was fine as long as cooking was done on a range or open fire alight all day whether or not food was cooking, but today lengthy cook-ups tend to mean large-size fuel bills – wasting money saved on ingredients. This is where the electric casserole comes in: it provides a modern method of slow cooking without running up a modern sized fuel bill. It also gives you delicious home cooked meals without tying you to the stove or kitchen sink. Ingredients come out as full of nourishment as they went in – you can be certain that vital nutrients are retained.

Small wonder the electric casserole, slow cooker or crock pot as it is also known is proving popular all over the world.

Slow cooking is the perfect answer for all sorts of people and situations. It's particularly useful if your work is busy but flexible – for example, if you have a free half hour in the *morning* to prepare a meal but no time (or energy!) later in the day. Busy housewives and mothers with children at school will find it a godsend for this reason.

The electric casserole takes the hassle out of entertaining too. You can relax and get ready in peace as though you were a guest at your own dinner party, knowing that the meal will be perfect without any last minute interference or worried excursions to the kitchen. You don't even have to start watching the clock as your guests fail to turn up on time – there'll be a delicious hot meal waiting for them whenever they arrive.

What exactly is an electric casserole and how does it work?

It's a casserole type of container made up of a metal or plastic outer casing with an earthen-ware inner container. There is a lid with a knob on top. The lid is either made of earthenware to match the inner container or plastic so that you can see what's going on inside.

The outer casing contains a heating element. This is usually wound round the side of the cooker so the food is totally surrounded by heat, not just heated from the base as in more conventional methods. The element thus en-sures an even gentle heat and there is no need to stir ingredients during cooking. The casserole has a handle situated at either side of the outer casing for lifting when not in use and the inner earthenware casserole also has handles if it is designed to be removed from the outer con-tainer (some are, some aren't).

Temperature controls Controls on all models are similar. There is a switch which can be set at HIGH or LOW. The low setting allows the food to cook for up to twelve hours without burning or sticking; the high setting cooks the food in about half the time. Some models have an indicator light to remind you that the appliance is turned on while others simply have an 'off' position.

Electric connection The casserole is connected to the mains by a straightforward electric lead. On some models the lead is removable so that the casserole can be lifted out and placed on the table for serving.

How it works When you switch the casserole on, the heating element inside the outer casing heats the inner earthenware casserole. The earthenware ensures even distribution of heat, which makes for even cooking all through. There is therefore no need to stir at all during cooking – in fact if you do lift the lid to stir, heat will be lost and the cooking time prolonged (see page 11). All cooking is done with the lid on. Condensation inside the lid runs down to form a liquid 'seal' around the lid rim and prevent evaporation.

Whichever setting you choose, high or low,

the food is heated (if it is not already hot enough) to a temperature high enough to destroy harmful bacteria and ensure that the correct temperature is maintained throughout the cooking time. You need therefore have no fears about undercooking or cooking at too low a temperature. As the food inside the casserole is usually kept just under boiling point it is sensitive to temperature changes, therefore *if you lift the lid the temperature of the food will drop*. As it can take as long as 30 minutes for food to regain the correct temperature it really is important not to look – even for a quick peep. If you are incurably inquisitive buy a casserole with a transparent lid (see 'Which model for you?' page 14).

Adding ingredients towards the end of the cooking time: you will notice that some recipes call for the addition of ingredients towards the end of the cooking time. Obviously this means lifting the lid and therefore extra time has been calculated to allow the casserole to return to the correct temperature. For example, pasta takes 45 minutes on the high setting after it has been added to the rest of the ingredients (see 'Adding pasta, dumplings and toppings', page 12).

How much fuel do you save?
An electric casserole will cook a complete all-in-one casserole meal for about one third of what it would cost you to cook the same dish in a conventional electric oven.

How versatile is it? What will it cook?
Electric casseroles make beautiful soups, both purées and substantial main meal soups. You can make a good old fashioned stock too – the gentle simmering ensures that all the flavour and goodness is retained. Electric casseroles will cook dried pulses, pasta and rice. Lentils, dried beans and dried split peas all need to be soaked overnight before you use them: if you don't soak them they won't soften and cook – even if your casserole is on for twelve hours. Pasta should be added towards the end of cooking time.

The gentle slow cooking turns cheaper tough-er cuts of meat or boiling fowl into succulent dishes fit for the most lavish dinner parties. You can pot roast all types of meat and bacon – the slow cooking and gentle heat prevent shrinkage so for once the meat comes out of the cooker almost the same size it went in.

Sponge and suet puddings cook beautifully, providing they are cooked entirely on the high setting. They come out light and fluffy with absolutely no bother.

Fruit cooks well and stays whole – even rhubarb is not reduced to the pulp so easily achieved by conventional methods.

Custards and milk puddings are creamy and do not curdle because they are cooked so slowly.

You can bake a very successful fruit cake in your electric casserole – either using a rich mixture or a simpler everyday version. The top of the cake does not come out quite as smooth as an oven baked cake but the texture and flavour are good.

Use your electric casserole to soften fruit for jam, marmalade and lemon curd, and to make fondues. You can even use it to keep a party punch or a mulled wine at the correct temperature.

Is there anything that can't be cooked in an electric casserole?
Because of the construction of the flesh, fish cooks quite quickly and will toughen if overcooked. For this reason the electric casserole isn't the best method of cooking fish – though it is possible (see Cod à la provençale on page 60, for example).

Cooking with your electric casserole

Preparing vegetables
Vegetables have a more dense composition than meat and for this reason they take much longer to cook in the electric casserole. Carrots may still be crunchy after 6 hours cooking so it is essential to cut vegetables into small pieces and arrange them around the sides and base of

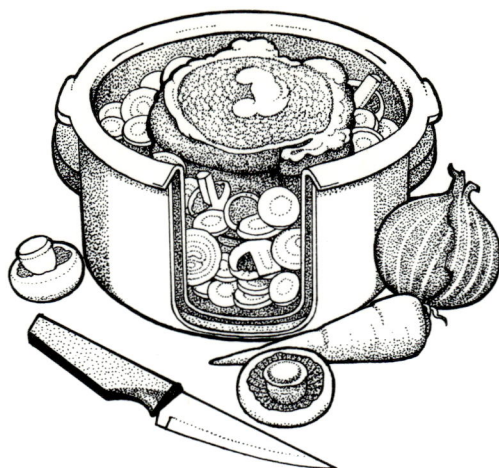

Packing the vegetables around the base and side of the electric casserole with the joint of meat in the centre.

the casserole with the meat on top. Vegetables that you would not normally add to a casserole until near the end of cooking time because they would overcook can be added to the electric casserole at the beginning of the cooking time: cauliflower florets, sliced courgettes, mushrooms, for example, will keep their shape and colour.

Frozen vegetables should be *completely* defrosted before being added to the electric casserole: if you add frozen vegetables to the casserole the cooking temperature drops drastically and you run the risk of bacteria multiplying. Dried peas, beans and pulses should be soaked for at least 12 hours or overnight and drained before adding to the electric casserole. If you don't soak dried pulses they may not cook through properly.

Preparing meat and poultry

All large pieces of fat should be trimmed from meat as the low cooking temperature will not melt fat but only reduce it to a soft unpleasant texture. All meat may be cut into cubes of about 3·5 cm (1½ in). Skin should be removed from chicken and duck before cooking but ready-cut portions do not need to be cut into smaller pieces. All frozen meat and poultry should be *completely* defrosted before cooking.

Pre-frying meat and vegetables

Some manufacturers state that pre-frying meat and vegetables is not necessary. A casserole can be made by placing cold raw ingredients into the electric casserole and pouring boiling stock over them but the result is anaemic in colour and insipid in flavour. Better results are achieved if the meat and vegetables are both pre-fried in a separate pan for 5–10 minutes (longer than normal, perhaps) until well-browned.

Adding stock and liquid

Stock or cooking liquid should be brought to the boil before being added to the electric casserole. This speeds up the time taken for the 'safe temperature' that destroys bacteria to be reached.

Adding pasta, dumplings and toppings

Although in general the lid of the electric casserole should not be lifted at all during cooking time, it is possible to add ingredients towards the end of cooking time providing the heat loss is taken into consideration. For both pasta and dumplings turn the control to the HIGH setting and add the pasta or dumplings to the electric casserole. Stir in pasta shapes and make sure dumplings are pushed under the level of the gravy or cooking liquid. Add such ingredients as quickly as possible and immediately replace the lid to prevent unnecessary loss of heat.

If you have a model with a removable earthenware inner casserole, you can add crumble or potato toppings at the end of the cooking time. Lift out the inner casserole, place the ingredients on top and brown under the grill or in the oven in the normal way. You can also cook, say, a steak and kidney pie in the electric casserole: cook the meat filling in the casserole, remove the inner casserole at the end of the cooking time, place the pastry lid on top and finish it in the oven.

Thickening gravy and sauces

You can toss meat in seasoned flour before pre-frying but it is also possible to thicken gravy and sauces at the end of the cooking process. To do this blend cornflour or flour to a smooth paste with a little cold water and stir into the electric casserole. If the dish has been cooked on the HIGH setting the cornflour will thicken immediately. If the dish has been cooked on the LOW setting, the lid may need to be replaced and cooking continued for about 10–15 minutes, until the sauce is thickened.

Adding cream
Fresh cream or soured cream can be added to dishes to enhance the flavour and improve the consistency of the sauce. Stir it in before serving or 15 minutes before the end of cooking time. Long cooking will cause cream to curdle.

Cooking in containers
Cook pâtés, sponges and suet puddings in heatproof glass or china basins and cakes in normal cake tins: place the basin or tin in the electric casserole with enough boiling water to come halfway up the side of the basin or tin – check that the container actually fits in before you start.

Cooking for freezing
The electric casserole is good for cooking food in quantity to freeze. Cool it quickly by pouring the hot cooked ingredients into another, cold container to chill. Pack and label in the normal way before freezing. Don't reheat cooked frozen food in the electric casserole: the low cooking temperature cannot heat the food fast enough for it to be safe.

Most recipes in the book will freeze easily without further preparation – we have marked these with a symbol (✤). Some recipes will need adapting. For example, cream and eggs should be added in a liaison after thawing and reheating; cornflour should be substituted for flour; pasta should be cooked separately and stirred into the reheated dish.

Adapting your favourite recipes
When adapting your own favourite recipes for cooking in the electric casserole it is useful to refer to similar recipes given in this book. Also read the manufacturer's directions carefully, and re-read this section on 'Cooking with your electric casserole'. The main thing to remember is that the amount of liquid is about two thirds of the normal quantity unless rice, pasta or pulses are to be added to the casserole towards the end of cooking time.

Test the food at the end of cooking time by piercing with a skewer or pointed knife. If longer cooking is required replace the lid and cook for *at least another hour.*

Cleaning your electric casserole
The principle of slow cooking at a low temperature means that food should not burn or stick to the inside of the earthenware casserole, so cleaning is minimal. Always switch off and unplug your electric casserole before cleaning. If your model has a *removable* earthenware inner casserole, wash the inner casserole in warm soapy water. Remember that earthenware is breakable and it is advisable not to fill the casserole with cold water immediately after cooking as the contrast in temperature could cause it to crack. Wipe the outer casing and the inner aluminium lining with a soft damp cloth and dry thoroughly. If stubborn stains occur, leave the casserole to soak in warm soapy water then scrub lightly with a plastic brush or nylon scouring pad. Don't try to scratch the

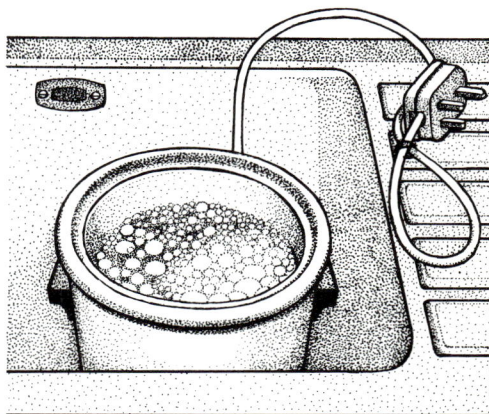

Stand the electric casserole in the sink to fill with hot soapy water – keep the flex on the draining board, secured with an elastic band.

food off or you may crack the glaze which would in turn trap food.

If your model does *not* have a removable earthenware casserole it cannot be immersed in water. Fold up the lead neatly and secure it with a rubber band to prevent it trailing in the sink. Place the electric casserole in an empty sink with the lead on the draining board. Fill the inner casserole with warm soapy water and leave to soak if necessary on the draining board. It is safest not to use the sink because of the danger of water getting into the works. Clean and dry thoroughly.

Which model for you?

Before buying an electric casserole it helps to decide which kind of dishes you expect to be cooking most often and in what quantities. If you live alone and don't go in much for entertaining it obviously makes sense to choose a smaller model than the one a mother of six children would go for. If you have a freezer, on the other hand, don't forget the time and money-saving aspect of cooking with an electric casserole. Recipes marked with a symbol (✤) are particularly easy to freeze. If you're catering for only one or two, it makes sense to have a cook-up once a week or so and freeze what you don't eat first time round in single or double portions.

The **Tower Slo-Cooker** [2439] has a brown aluminium outer casing with an integral brown earthenware casserole, so it cannot be totally immersed for washing. It has a detachable lead. A good size for the average family of four although the narrow diameter of the casserole determines the size of pudding basin that can be used.

Controls: HIGH/LOW rocker switch with no indicator light
Electrical loading: HIGH – 120 watts; LOW – 60 watts
Capacity: 2 litres (3 ½ pints)

The larger **Tower Slo-Cooker** [2761] has a mushroom-coloured plastic outer casing with moulded handles. The integral earthenware casserole is brown with a matching lid. The lead is detachable. It is suitable for larger families or those who entertain in numbers or cook double quantities and put half in the freezer.

Controls: HIGH/LOW rocker switch with an indicator light
Electrical loading: HIGH – 130 watts; LOW – 75 watts
Capacity: 3·5 litres (6 pints)

The **Prestige Crock-Pot** [L8100] has the smallest capacity. The outer casing is made from orange polyester with moulded handles and an aluminium lining. The brown earthenware inner casserole and lid are removable so can be taken to the table or dishes can be browned under the grill or in the oven. This casserole has a heating element in the base of the outer casing and not wound around the sides. A good size for the family of four. The shallow earthenware casserole determines the size of pudding basin that can be used.

Controls: HIGH/LOW rocker switch that is also an indicator light
Electrical loading: HIGH – 160 watts; LOW – 115 watts
Capacity: 1·8 litres (3 ¼ pints)

The **Kenwood Cook-Pot** [A135] has a rigid texture plastic outer casing, available in orange or green, with an aluminium lining. The earthenware inner casserole is brown with an amber smoked plastic lid so you can see the food cooking. The inner casserole is removable so can be taken to the table or dishes can be browned under the grill or in the oven. The lead is detachable. It is not quite as large as the larger Tower model but it will take six servings of most dishes. The extra depth of the earthenware casserole makes it a good size for larger pudding basins.

Controls: HIGH/LOW/OFF rocker switch with no indicator light
Electrical loading: HIGH – 170 watts; LOW – 70 watts
Capacity: 3·2 litres (5 ½ pints)

Tower Slo-Cooker (2439)   Tower Slo-Cooker (2761)   Prestige Crock-Pot (L8100)

Kenwood Cook-Pot (A135)   Dee Gee Crockery Chef (68)   Pifco Slow Cooker

The **Dee Gee Crockery Chef [68]** is taller and narrower than most models. The outer casing is mustard-coloured metal with the name of the cooker written in large letters across it. The integral brown earthenware inner casserole is fitted with a smoked plastic lid. The lead is not detachable. The narrow diameter of the casserole, 18 cm (7 in), limits the use of pudding basins and cake tins.

Controls: HIGH/LOW/OFF knob without an indicator light
Electrical loading: HIGH – 140 watts; LOW – 70 watts
Capacity: 3 litres (5¼ pints)

The **Pifco Slow Cooker** has an outer casing of red steel with a brown earthenware casserole that is removable. It has a clear glassware lid so that you can see what is happening but this should be carefully placed in position to prevent evaporation. The lead is not detachable. The HIGH setting is hotter than most other models.

Controls: HIGH/LOW/OFF knob with an indicator light situated above
Electrical loading: HIGH – 260 watts; LOW – 260 watts with thermostat control
Capacity: 2·8 litres (5 pints)

DOS AND DON'TS

Do read your manufacturer's instruction leaflet carefully before starting and follow any special points. For example, Tower recommend you to preheat their models on HIGH for about 20 minutes before adding any food.

Do follow the recipe instructions carefully – bearing in mind the manufacturer's instructions.

Do cut vegetables into small pieces.

Do defrost vegetables completely before adding them to the casserole.

Do trim away all excess fat from pieces of meat.

Do soak dried vegetables and pulses overnight or for at least 12 hours before cooking. Drain before adding to the casserole.

Do pre-fry meat and vegetables for the best results.

Do make sure stock or liquid is boiling before you add it to the casserole.

Do add pasta or dumplings as quickly as possible, to avoid unnecessary heat loss.

Do check that pudding basins or cake tins will fit easily into the casserole without touching the sides before filling them with ingredients.

Do add *boiling* water to the casserole when cooking puddings, pâtés and cakes.

Do turn off and unplug the casserole before cleaning.

Do fold and secure the lead before washing integral casseroles.

Don't be tempted to lift the lid and see how the food is cooking.

Don't stir the food during cooking.

Don't add frozen food to the casserole.

Don't add dried vegetables and pulses to the casserole without soaking them first.

Don't add cream to the casserole until the end of cooking time or as directed in the recipes.

Don't reheat cooked frozen foods in the casserole.

Don't scrape surplus food from the casserole before washing it.

Don't immerse integral casseroles in water.

Don't fill hot casseroles with cold water.

Don't fill your casserole right to the top: leave 2·5 cm (1 in) at the top of the earthenware casserole.

Soups

✤ Brown or meat stock

1–1½ kg (2–3 lb) bones from cooked or raw meat
1 onion, skinned and sliced
25 g (1 oz) lard
1 stick of celery, washed and sliced
2·5 ml (½ level tsp) salt
4 peppercorns

For a really brown stock cook the bones and onion in the fat in a frying pan for 10–15 minutes until golden brown. Drain well and place in the electric casserole with the celery and seasoning. Pour enough boiling water over the bones to cover them. Place the lid in position and cook on low for 10–12 hours or overnight.

Strain the stock, leave to cool and skim off any fat.

✤ Chicken stock

1 chicken carcass, fresh or cooked
chicken giblets
1 onion, skinned and chopped
1 carrot, peeled and chopped
1 stick of celery, washed and sliced
2·5 ml (½ level tsp) salt
4 peppercorns
bouquet garni (optional)

Break up the carcass and place in the electric casserole with the remaining ingredients and enough boiling water to cover. Place the lid in position and cook on low for 10–12 hours or overnight.

Strain the stock, leave to cool and skim off any fat.

✤ Vegetable stock

100 g (4 oz) onions, skinned and chopped
100 g (4 oz) carrots, peeled and chopped
2 sticks of celery, washed and sliced
50 g (2 oz) swede or turnip, peeled and chopped
bouquet garni (optional)
2·5 ml (½ level tsp) salt
4 peppercorns

Place all the ingredients in the electric casserole with enough boiling water to cover the vegetables. Place the lid in position and cook on low for 6–8 hours or overnight.

Remove any scum, strain and leave to cool.

✤ Creamed vegetable broth

225 g (8 oz) potatoes, peeled
225 g (8 oz) swede, peeled
225 g (8 oz) turnip, peeled
225 g (8 oz) carrots, peeled
100 g (4 oz) parsnips, peeled
2 leeks, washed and sliced
2 sticks of celery, washed
1 large onion, skinned
25 g (1 oz) butter
30 ml (2 level tbsp) flour
900 ml (1½ pints) chicken stock
300 ml (½ pint) milk
1 bayleaf
2·5 ml (½ level tsp) salt
freshly ground pepper

Roughly chop all the vegetables. Melt the butter in a saucepan and cook the vegetables for 5 minutes until golden brown. Stir in the flour and cook for a further 1 minute. Add the stock, milk, bayleaf and seasoning and bring to the boil. Pour into the electric casserole, place the lid in position and cook on high for 3–4 hours or on low for 6–8 hours.

MAKES ABOUT 1·7 LITRES (3 PINTS)

✤ Cidered celery soup

Quick to prepare, economical, easy to freeze

1 head of celery, washed
1 large carrot, peeled
1 medium-sized onion, skinned
2 large potatoes, peeled
1 large cooking apple, peeled and cored
900 ml (1½ pints) chicken stock
400 ml (¾ pint) dry cider
salt and freshly ground pepper

Chop all the vegetables and apple finely. Place them in the electric casserole with the stock, cider and seasoning and stir well. Place the lid in

Cidered celery soup

position and cook on high for 3–4 hours or low for 6–8 hours. Purée the vegetables in a blender or rub through a sieve. Reheat in a pan if necessary.

MAKES ABOUT 1·7 LITRES (3 PINTS)

✤ Hearty corn chowder

ILLUSTRATED IN COLOUR FACING PAGE 48

15 ml (1 tbsp) vegetable oil
100 g (4 oz) streaky bacon, rinded and chopped
1 green pepper, seeded and chopped
2 sticks of celery, washed and chopped
1 large onion, skinned and chopped
175 g (6 oz) potatoes, peeled and chopped
100 g (4 oz) button mushrooms
50 g (2 oz) flour
400 ml (¾ pint) chicken stock
568 ml (1 pint) milk
salt and freshly ground pepper
1 bayleaf
5 ml (1 level tsp) ground nutmeg
326-g (11½-oz) can sweetcorn
grated Parmesan cheese and freshly chopped
    parsley to garnish

Heat the oil in a saucepan and cook the bacon for 10 minutes until crisp. Remove from the pan and reserve. Add the vegetables to the pan and cook for 5 minutes until golden brown. Stir in the flour and cook for 1 minute. Stir in the stock, milk, seasoning, bayleaf and nutmeg and bring to the boil. Stir in the sweetcorn and bacon and pour into the electric casserole. Place the lid in position and cook on high for 2–3 hours or low for 4–6 hours. Serve sprinkled with Parmesan cheese and freshly chopped parsley.

MAKES ABOUT 1·4 LITRES (2½ PINTS)

✤ Creamed tomato and orange soup

25 g (1 oz) butter
1 medium-sized onion, skinned and chopped
2 sticks of celery, washed and chopped
900 g (2 lb) tomatoes, skinned and chopped
grated rind and juice of 1 orange
15 ml (1 level tbsp) flour
600 ml (1 pint) chicken stock
1·25 ml (¼ level tsp) dried rosemary
salt and freshly ground pepper
2·5 ml (½ level tsp) sugar
45 ml (3 tbsp) cream or top of the milk and
    chopped fresh chives to serve

Melt the butter in a large saucepan and fry the onion and celery for 5 minutes until soft. Add the remaining ingredients except the cream and chives. Pour into the electric casserole, place the lid in position and cook on high for 2–3 hours or low for 4–6 hours.

Before serving, pour a swirl of cream on each helping and sprinkle with chives.

MAKES ABOUT 1·1 LITRES (2 PINTS)

✤ French onion soup

This classic French onion soup recipe topped with cheese and toast has been specially adapted for the electric casserole

40 g (1½ oz) butter
450 g (1 lb) onions, skinned and sliced
30 ml (2 level tbsp) flour
900 ml (1½ pints) beef stock
salt and freshly ground pepper
1 bayleaf
100 g (4 oz) Gruyère cheese, grated and 1 French
    loaf, sliced to serve

Melt the butter in a large saucepan and fry the onions for 10–15 minutes until well browned. Stir in the flour and cook for a further 2–3 minutes. Add the stock, seasoning, and bayleaf and bring to the boil. Pour into the electric casserole, place the lid in position and cook on high for 3–4 hours or low for 6–8 hours.

Sprinkle the cheese on top of the bread and cook under a hot grill until golden brown. Place on top of the soup and serve at once.
MAKES ABOUT 1·1 LITRES (2 PINTS)

✤ Vegetable soup with bacon dumplings

ILLUSTRATED IN COLOUR ON THE JACKET

Delicious winter vegetables flavoured with cider and served with fluffy bacon dumplings

50 g (2 oz) butter
1 large onion, skinned and chopped
2 large carrots, peeled and chopped
2 leeks, washed and sliced
1 medium-sized swede, peeled and chopped
1 turnip, peeled and chopped
2 sticks of celery, washed and chopped
1 large cooking apple, peeled, cored and chopped
30 ml (2 level tbsp) flour
600 ml (1 pint) chicken stock
300 ml (½ pint) dry cider
salt and freshly ground pepper
bouquet garni

For the dumplings
50 g (2 oz) self raising flour
25 g (1 oz) shredded suet
½ small onion, skinned and finely chopped
50 g (2 oz) streaky bacon, rinded and finely chopped
salt and freshly ground pepper

Melt the butter in a large saucepan and fry the vegetables and apple for 5 minutes until lightly browned. Stir in the flour and gradually add the stock and cider. Bring to the boil and season well. Pour into the electric casserole, add the bouquet garni and place the lid in position. Cook on high for 3–4 hours or low for 6–8 hours.

To make the dumplings: stir the dry in-gredients, onion and bacon together and add enough water to mix to a soft dough. Roll into

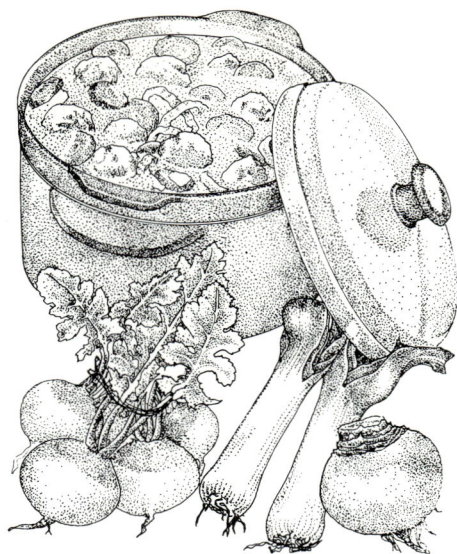

Vegetable soup with bacon dumplings

small balls. 30 minutes before the end of cooking time turn the electric casserole to high. Add the dumplings, pushing them under the liquid and continue cooking.
MAKES ABOUT 1·1 LITRES (2 PINTS)
Freeze without the dumplings

✤ Minestrone soup

This classic recipe has been specially adapted for the electric casserole. Serve with toast triangles to make a more filling meal

25 g (1 oz) haricot beans, soaked overnight
15 ml (1 tbsp) vegetable oil
1 leek, washed and sliced
1 medium-sized onion, skinned and chopped
1 clove of garlic, skinned and crushed
1 stick of celery, washed and chopped
1 carrot, peeled and sliced
2 rashers streaky bacon, rinded and chopped
1·1 litres (2 pints) chicken stock
25 g (1 oz) shortcut macaroni
225 g (8 oz) tomatoes, skinned and chopped
salt and freshly ground pepper
grated Parmesan cheese to garnish

Soak the haricot beans overnight and drain.

Heat the oil in a saucepan and cook the vegetables and bacon for 5 minutes until soft. Stir in the stock, macaroni, haricot beans, tomatoes and seasoning. Bring to the boil, pour into the electric casserole and stir well. Place the lid in position and cook on high for 3–4 hours or low for 6–8 hours. Just before serving sprinkle with cheese.

MAKES ABOUT 1·4 LITRES (2½ PINTS)

Freeze without the pasta

✤ Green pea and bacon soup

900 g (2 lb) fresh peas, shelled, or 225 g (8 oz) dried green peas, soaked overnight
50 g (2 oz) butter
1 small onion, skinned and chopped
225 g (8 oz) streaky bacon, rinded and finely chopped
50 g (2 oz) flour
568 ml (1 pint) milk
400 ml (¾ pint) chicken stock
salt and freshly ground pepper
freshly chopped parsley to garnish

If you are using dried peas, soak them overnight and drain. Melt the butter in a large saucepan. Cook the onion and bacon for 5 minutes until soft. Stir in the flour and gradually add the milk and stock. Bring to the boil and add the peas and seasoning. Pour into the electric casserole and place the lid in position. Cook on high for 3–4 hours or low for 6–8 hours. Serve sprinkled with parsley.

MAKES ABOUT 1·4 LITRES (2½ PINTS)

Country lentil soup

ILLUSTRATED IN COLOUR FACING PAGE 48

700 g (1½ lb) hock or knuckle bacon joint, soaked overnight
225 g (8 oz) red lentils, soaked overnight
2 large carrots, peeled and sliced
2 sticks of celery, washed and sliced
1 large onion, skinned and chopped
15 ml (1 tbsp) Worcestershire sauce
30 ml (2 level tbsp) tomato paste
1·4 litres (2½ pints) chicken stock
freshly ground pepper

Soak the joint and the lentils overnight and

drain. Place all the ingredients in the electric casserole, place the lid in position and cook on high for 4–5 hours or low for 8–10 hours.

Remove the bacon joint from the soup, flake off the meat and reserve. Leave the vegetables whole or purée in a blender or rub through a sieve. Reheat the vegetables and bacon together in a saucepan.

MAKES ABOUT 1·4 LITRES (2½ PINTS)

✤ Cock-a-leekie

This much-loved Scottish soup is especially easy in the electric casserole

1·1 kg (2½ lb) boiling chicken, jointed
1·1 litres (2 pints) chicken stock
450 g (1 lb) leeks, sliced and washed
225 g (8 oz) dried prunes
2·5 ml (½ level tsp) mixed herbs
salt and freshly ground pepper

Place the chicken in the electric casserole and pour the stock over it. Add the remaining ingredients, place the lid in position and cook on high for 4–5 hours or low for 8–10 hours.

Remove the chicken from the soup, remove the meat from the joints and cut into fairly large pieces. Stir the meat into the soup before serving. Reheat if necessary.

MAKES ABOUT 1·4 LITRES (2½ PINTS)

Butter bean soup

225 g (8 oz) butter beans, soaked overnight
25 g (1 oz) butter
2 sticks of celery, washed and chopped
1 onion, skinned and sliced
25 g (1 oz) flour
300 ml (½ pint) water
400 ml (¾ pint) milk
salt and freshly ground pepper
1 bayleaf
1 egg
30 ml (2 tbsp) cream or top of the milk
1 large tomato, skinned and chopped
freshly chopped parsley to garnish

Soak the beans overnight and drain. Melt the butter in a saucepan and cook the celery and onion for 2–3 minutes. Stir in the flour and cook for a further 1 minute. Stir in the water, milk, seasoning, bayleaf and butter beans and bring to the boil. Pour into the electric casserole, place the lid in position and cook on high for 3–4 hours or low for 6–8 hours.

5 minutes before the end of cooking time, beat the egg and cream together and stir into the soup with the tomato. Replace the lid and continue cooking. Serve sprinkled with parsley.
MAKES ABOUT 1·1 LITRES (2 PINTS)

✤ Golden pea and ham soup

An old fashioned family favourite

275 g (10 oz) split peas, soaked overnight
275 g (10 oz) lean hock or knuckle joint
1·1 litres (2 pints) chicken stock
1 onion, skinned and chopped
2 leeks, washed and chopped
1 stick of celery, washed and chopped
1 bayleaf
salt and freshly ground pepper

Soak the split peas overnight and drain. Place all the ingredients except the bacon joint in the electric casserole and stir well. Add the bacon joint. Place the lid in position and cook on high for 4–5 hours or low for 8–10 hours.

Just before serving remove the bacon joint, flake off the meat and reserve. Purée the vegetables in a blender or by rubbing through a sieve. Return to the electric casserole with the bacon, stirring well.
MAKES ABOUT 1·4 LITRES (2½ PINTS)

✤ Chilli bean soup

225 g (8 oz) red kidney beans, soaked overnight
15 ml (1 tbsp) vegetable oil
1 large onion, skinned and chopped
225 g (8 oz) minced beef
425 g (15-oz) can tomatoes
30 ml (2 level tbsp) tomato paste
5–10 ml (1–2 tsp) chilli seasoning
15 ml (1 tbsp) Worcestershire sauce
salt and freshly ground pepper
15 ml (1 level tbsp) plain flour
600 ml (1 pint) beef stock

Chilli bean soup

Soak the beans overnight and drain. Heat the oil in a pan and cook the onion for 5 minutes until soft. Add the mince and cook for 5 minutes until browned. Stir in the beans, tomatoes, tomato paste, chilli seasoning, Worcestershire sauce and seasoning. Stir in the flour and gradually add the stock. Bring to the boil, stirring, and pour into the electric casserole. Place the lid in position and cook on high for 3–4 hours or low for 6–8 hours.
MAKES ABOUT 900 ML (1½ PINTS)

Chicken noodle soup

A main meal soup to serve with savoury cheese scones for lunch or supper

25 g (1 oz) butter
15 ml (1 tbsp) vegetable oil
1 medium-sized onion, skinned and chopped
2 sticks of celery, washed and chopped
2 carrots, peeled and chopped
325 g (12 oz) chicken, chopped
30 ml (2 level tbsp) flour
1·1 litres (2 pints) chicken stock
salt and freshly ground pepper
100 g (4 oz) noodles
freshly chopped parsley to garnish

Heat the butter and oil in a large saucepan and fry the onion, celery, carrots and chicken for 5–10 minutes until golden brown. Add the flour and gradually stir in the stock. Bring to the boil and season well. Pour into the electric casserole and place the lid in position. Cook on high for 3–4 hours or low for 6–8 hours.

45 minutes before the end of cooking time, turn the electric casserole to high and stir in the noodles. Replace the lid and continue cooking. Serve sprinkled with parsley.

MAKES ABOUT 1·4 LITRES (2 ½ PINTS)

✤ Oxtail and vegetable soup

Oxtail soup made easy with the electric casserole

25 g (1 oz) butter or lard
1 large oxtail, trimmed and jointed
1 large onion, skinned and chopped
1 large carrot, peeled and sliced
2 sticks of celery, washed and chopped
2 medium-sized potatoes, peeled and chopped
100 g (4 oz) flat mushrooms, sliced
45 ml (3 level tbsp) flour
1·1 litres (2 pints) beef stock
15 ml (1 tbsp) Worcestershire sauce
15 ml (1 level tbsp) tomato paste
2·5 ml (½ level tsp) dried mixed herbs
salt and freshly ground pepper

Heat the fat in a saucepan and cook the oxtail for 10 minutes until golden brown. Remove and place in the electric casserole. Add the vegetables to the pan and cook for 5 minutes until golden brown. Remove from the pan and add to the electric casserole. Stir the flour into the pan juices and gradually add the stock. Bring to the boil, stirring, and add the Worcestershire sauce, tomato paste, herbs and seasoning and pour over the browned oxtail and vegetables in the electric casserole. Place the lid in position and cook on high for 3–4 hours or low for 6–8 hours.

Just before serving flake the meat off the bone and stir into the soup.
MAKES ABOUT 2 LITRES (3 ½ PINTS)
Flake the meat off the bone before freezing

✤ Spicy tomato soup

Serve with bacon sandwiches for lunch or supper

30 ml (2 tbsp) vegetable oil
1 large carrot, peeled and sliced
1 large onion, skinned and chopped
175 g (6 oz) potatoes, peeled and chopped
2 leeks, washed and sliced
450 g (1 lb) tomatoes, skinned and chopped
1·25 ml (¼ level tsp) ground mace
1 bayleaf
1·25 ml (¼ level tsp) allspice
salt and freshly ground pepper
5 ml (1 level tsp) caster sugar
60 ml (4 level tbsp) tomato paste
grated rind of ½ lemon
1·1 litres (2 pints) chicken stock
ground nutmeg and freshly chopped parsley to garnish

Heat the oil in a saucepan and cook the vegetables for 5 minutes until golden brown. Stir in the tomatoes, all the seasonings, sugar, tomato paste, lemon rind and stock. Bring to the boil, stirring, and pour into the electric casserole. Place the lid in position and cook on high for 3–4 hours or on low for 6–8 hours.

Purée in a blender or rub through a sieve and reheat if necessary. Serve sprinkled with nutmeg and parsley.
MAKES ABOUT 2 LITRES (3 ½ PINTS)

✤ Haricot bean and tomato soup

175 g (6 oz) haricot beans, soaked overnight
30 ml (2 tbsp) vegetable oil
1 large onion, skinned and chopped
100 g (4 oz) streaky bacon, rinded and chopped
45 ml (3 level tbsp) flour
900 ml (1 ½ pints) chicken stock
450 g (1 lb) tomatoes, skinned and chopped
30 ml (2 level tbsp) tomato paste
1 bayleaf
15 ml (1 tbsp) Worcestershire sauce
salt and freshly ground pepper

Soak the beans overnight and drain. Heat the oil in a large saucepan and fry the onion for 10 minutes until golden brown. Add the bacon and fry gently for 5 minutes. Remove from the pan and place in the electric casserole. Stir the flour into the remaining oil and gradually add the stock. Add the remaining ingredients, bring to the boil and pour into the electric casserole. Place the lid in position and cook on high for 3–4 hours or low for 6–8 hours.

MAKES ABOUT 1·1 LITRES (2 PINTS)

✤ Cream of carrot and leek soup

We have suggested puréeing this delicious warming soup, but it can be served as it is

700 g (1½ lb) carrots, peeled and sliced
1 stick of celery, washed and chopped
6 small leeks, washed and chopped
1 bayleaf
6 parsley sprigs
1·4 litres (2½ pints) chicken stock
1·25 ml (¼ level tsp) ground nutmeg
salt and freshly ground white pepper
grated rind of ½ lemon
2·5 ml (½ level tsp) brown sugar
142-ml (5-fl oz) carton single cream
freshly chopped parsley and croûtons to garnish

Place the vegetables, herbs, stock, nutmeg and seasoning in the electric casserole. Place the lid in position and cook on high for 3–4 hours or low for 6–8 hours. Purée the vegetables in a blender or rub through a sieve. Reheat, stir in the lemon rind, sugar and cream and garnish with chopped parsley and croûtons.

MAKES ABOUT 1·7 LITRES (3 PINTS)

Freeze without the cream

Garlic sausage soup

15 ml (1 tbsp) vegetable oil
100 g (4 oz) garlic sausage, cubed
1 onion, skinned and chopped
1 clove of garlic, skinned and crushed
225 g (8 oz) tomatoes, skinned and chopped
1 cooking apple, peeled, cored and chopped
salt and freshly ground pepper
15 ml (1 level tbsp) tomato paste
15 ml (1 tbsp) Worcestershire sauce
15 ml (1 level tbsp) flour
1·4 litres (2½ pints) chicken stock
100 g (4 oz) small pasta shapes

Heat the oil in a saucepan and fry the garlic sausage, onion, garlic, tomatoes and apple for 2–3 minutes until softened. Season well and add the tomato paste and Worcestershire sauce. Stir in the flour and gradually add the stock. Bring to the boil and pour into the electric casserole. Place the lid in position and cook on high for 3–4 hours or low for 6–8 hours.

45 minutes before the end of cooking time turn the electric casserole to high, stir in the pasta shapes, replace the lid and continue cooking.

MAKES ABOUT 1·4 LITRES (2½ PINTS)

✤ Spiced beef and vegetable soup

This is a substantial soup with a hint of curry

15 g (½ oz) butter
1 small onion, skinned and chopped
1 small carrot, peeled and chopped
1 small turnip, peeled and sliced
1 small cooking apple, peeled, cored and chopped
325 g (12 oz) shin beef, cut into 2-cm (¾-in) cubes
15 ml (1 level tbsp) flour
10 ml (2 level tsp) curry powder
1·1 litres (2 pints) beef stock
bouquet garni
7·5 ml (1½ level tsp) salt
freshly ground pepper
5 ml (1 level tsp) chutney
25 g (1 oz) long grain rice
10 ml (2 tsp) lemon juice
30 ml (2 tbsp) cream or top of the milk

Melt the butter in a saucepan, add the vegetables and apple and cook for 5 minutes, until soft. Place in the electric casserole. Add the meat to the pan and cook for 5 minutes until browned. Place in the electric casserole. Add the flour and curry powder to the pan and cook for 1 minute. Gradually stir in the stock, bouquet garni, seasoning, chutney and rice and bring to the boil. Pour into the electric casserole and stir well. Place the lid in position and cook on high for 3–4 hours or low for 6–8 hours.

Just before serving stir in the lemon juice and cream.

MAKES ABOUT 1·1 LITRES (2 PINTS)

Freeze without the cream

Sausage and lentil soup

This is a good filling soup for hungry children

100 g (4 oz) lentils, soaked overnight
25 g (1 oz) butter
225 g (8 oz) pork or beef sausages
1 large onion, skinned and chopped
2 sticks of celery, washed and diced
1 small turnip, peeled and diced
175 g (6 oz) potatoes, peeled and diced
1 large cooking apple, peeled, cored and chopped
1·1 litres (2 pints) beef stock
1 bayleaf
5 ml (1 level tsp) paprika
salt and freshly ground pepper

Soak the lentils overnight in cold water and drain. Melt the butter in a frying pan and cook the sausages for 5–10 minutes until golden brown all over. Remove from the pan, slice into 1-cm (½-in) pieces and place in the electric casserole. Cook the vegetables and apple in the remaining fat for 5 minutes, until golden brown. Add the lentils, stock, bayleaf and seasoning and bring to the boil. Pour into the electric casserole. Place the lid in position and cook on high for 3–4 hours or low for 6–8 hours.
MAKES ABOUT 900 ML (2 PINTS)

✢ Scotch broth

This makes two meals: serve the broth with the meat first, then save the remaining vegetable broth for another day

700 g (1½ lb) middle neck of lamb
1 carrot, peeled and finely sliced
1 potato, peeled and chopped
1 leek, thinly sliced and washed
1 onion, skinned and chopped
45 ml (3 level tbsp) pearl barley
1·7 litres (3 pints) boiling water
10 ml (2 level tsp) salt
freshly ground black pepper

Cut the lamb into neat 2-cm (¾-in) cubes. Remove any excess fat. Fry without additional fat in a large pan for about 10 minutes until browned. Drain the lamb and reserve. Fry the vegetables for 5 minutes until beginning to soften. Drain off any excess fat. Transfer the lamb and vegetables to the electric casserole, add the pearl barley, boiling water and seasoning. Mix well together. Place the lid in position and cook on high for 4–6 hours or low for 8 hours or overnight.
MAKES ABOUT 1·7 LITRES (3 PINTS)

✢ Chicken and lemon soup

A summer creamy chicken soup with slices of courgette that stay crunchy

50 g (2 oz) butter
450 g (1 lb) chicken, diced
1 small onion, skinned and chopped
2 sticks of celery, washed and chopped
2 courgettes, trimmed and sliced
30 ml (2 level tbsp) flour
grated rind and juice of 1 lemon
2·5 ml (½ level tsp) sugar
600 ml (1 pint) chicken stock
salt and freshly ground pepper
142-ml (5-fl oz) carton soured cream

Melt the butter in a large saucepan and fry the chicken and onion for 10 minutes. Add the celery and courgettes and cook for a further 2–3 minutes. Stir in the flour and gradually add the lemon juice, rind, sugar and stock. Bring to the boil and season. Pour into the electric casserole, place the lid in position and cook on high for 3–4 hours or low for 6–8 hours. Just before serving, stir in the cream.
MAKES ABOUT 1·1 LITRES (2 PINTS)
Freeze without the cream

✢ Cauliflower soup with cheese

The cauliflower florets stay whole and pleasantly crisp even after many hours of cooking

50 g (2 oz) butter
1 small onion, skinned and chopped
50 g (2 oz) streaky bacon, rinded and chopped
2 carrots, peeled and sliced
30 ml (2 level tbsp) flour
568 ml (1 pint) milk
300 ml (½ pint) chicken stock
1 bayleaf
salt and freshly ground pepper
1 large cauliflower, divided into florets
100 g (4 oz) Double Gloucester cheese, grated

Melt the butter in a large saucepan. Fry the onion, bacon and carrot for 3–5 minutes. Stir in the flour and gradually add the milk and stock. Bring to the boil and add the remaining ingredients except the cheese. Pour into the electric casserole and place the lid in position. Cook on high for 3–4 hours, or low for 6–8 hours.

Just before serving stir in the cheese.
MAKES ABOUT 1 LITRE (1¾ PINTS)

Bean, bacon and courgette soup

Serve with hot garlic bread for lunch or supper

100 g (4 oz) haricot beans, soaked overnight
30 ml (2 tbsp) vegetable oil
50 g (2 oz) butter
900 g (2 lb) potatoes, peeled and chopped
225 g (8 oz) courgettes, trimmed and sliced
225 g (8 oz) leeks, washed and sliced
3 sticks of celery, washed and chopped
225 g (8 oz) streaky bacon, rinded and chopped
25 g (1 oz) flour
1·1 litres (2 pints) chicken stock
salt and freshly ground pepper
2·5 ml (½ level tsp) dried mixed herbs
2·5 ml (½ level tsp) paprika
grated Parmesan cheese and freshly chopped parsley to garnish

Soak the beans overnight and drain. Heat the oil and butter together in a large saucepan and cook the prepared vegetables and bacon for 10 minutes until golden brown. Stir in the flour and cook for 1 minute. Gradually stir in the stock, seasoning, herbs, paprika and beans. Bring to the boil, stirring, and pour into the electric casserole. Place the lid in position and cook on high for 3–4 hours or low for 6–8 hours. Serve sprinkled with cheese and parsley.
MAKES ABOUT 1·7 LITRES (3 PINTS)

Pot au feu

This classic recipe has been specially adapted for the electric casserole. Slice the meat and serve it with a little of the soup or gravy. Serve the soup the next day

700 g (1½ lb) brisket or topside
15 ml (1 tbsp) vegetable oil
2 large carrots, peeled and sliced
1 turnip, peeled and sliced
1 onion, skinned and sliced
1 parsnip, peeled and sliced
1 leek, washed and sliced
2 sticks of celery, washed and sliced
½ small cabbage, shredded
1·4 litres (2½ pints) beef stock
salt and freshly ground pepper
bouquet garni
15 ml (1 level tbsp) tapioca

Tie the meat securely with string to keep it in shape while cooking.

Heat the oil in a frying pan and cook the meat for 5–10 minutes until all sides are well browned. Remove from the pan and reserve. Add the

Pot au feu

vegetables to the pan and cook for 5–10 minutes, stir in the stock, seasoning, bouquet garni and tapioca. Bring to the boil and pour into the electric casserole. Place the meat in the electric casserole. Place the lid in position and cook on high for 3–4 hours or low for 6–8 hours.
MAKES ABOUT 1·7 LITRES (3 PINTS)

Curried lamb soup

25 g (1 oz) butter
1 large onion, skinned and chopped
1 small green pepper, seeded and chopped
325 g (12 oz) lean stewing lamb, cut into 1-cm (½-in) cubes
10–15 ml (2–3 tsp) curry powder
2·5 ml (½ level tsp) paprika
900 ml (1½ pints) chicken stock
50 g (2 oz) long grain rice
1 large cooking apple, peeled, cored and chopped
50 g (2 oz) sultanas
1 large ripe tomato, skinned and chopped
salt and freshly ground pepper

Melt the butter in a large saucepan and cook the onion and pepper for 5 minutes until soft. Add the lamb and cook for 5–10 minutes until browned. Stir in the curry powder and paprika and cook for 1 minute. Stir in the stock, rice, apple, sultanas, tomato and seasoning. Bring to the boil and pour into the electric casserole. Place the lid in position and cook on high for 3–4 hours or low for 6–8 hours.
MAKES ABOUT 1·1 LITRES (2 PINTS)

✢ Curry soup

A delicately flavoured curry soup to serve for the family or swirled with cream at a dinner party

45 ml (3 level tbsp) flour
15 ml (1 level tbsp) curry paste
150 ml (¼ pint) cold water
1 litre (1¾ pints) hot chicken stock
1 medium-sized onion, skinned and chopped
30 ml (2 level tbsp) ground almonds
30 ml (2 level tbsp) desiccated coconut
50 g (2 oz) seedless raisins
strip of lemon rind
1 bayleaf
15 ml (1 level tbsp) cornflour

Mix the flour and curry paste together and blend to a smooth paste with the cold water. Pour the hot stock on to the paste and stir well. Pour the mixture into the electric casserole with the onion, almonds, coconut, raisins, lemon rind and bayleaf. Place the lid in position and cook on high for 2–3 hours or on low for 4–6 hours.

One hour before the end of cooking time, blend the cornflour to a smooth paste with a little water and add a little soup to the mixture, stirring. Return the blended mixture to the soup and stir in. Replace the lid and continue cooking.
MAKES ABOUT 1·1 LITRES (2 PINTS)

✢ Mulligatawny soup

This is a substantial vegetable soup to serve for lunch or supper. It has a traditional curry flavour and creamy texture

25 g (1 oz) butter
2 large onions, skinned and chopped
1 carrot, peeled and chopped
1 small turnip, peeled and chopped
1 cooking apple, peeled, cored and chopped
50 g (2 oz) streaky bacon, rinded and chopped
15 ml (1 level tbsp) curry powder
15 ml (1 level tbsp) curry paste
50 g (2 oz) plain flour
1 litre (1¾ pints) beef stock
bouquet garni
salt and freshly ground pepper
5 ml (1 tsp) lemon juice
30 ml (2 tbsp) single cream or top of the milk

Melt the butter in a large saucepan and cook the vegetables, apple and bacon for 5 minutes until soft. Stir in the curry powder, curry paste and flour and cook for 1 minute. Gradually stir in the stock and bring to the boil, stirring. Add the bouquet garni and seasoning and pour into the electric casserole. Place the lid in position and cook on high for 3–4 hours or low for 6–8 hours.

Just before serving stir in the lemon juice and cream.
MAKES ABOUT 1·4 LITRES (2½ PINTS)
Freeze without the cream

✤ Sherried kidney soup

A delicious kidney soup to serve with crusty granary bread for lunch or supper

100 g (4 oz) kidneys, washed
15 g (½ oz) butter
1 carrot, peeled and diced
1 small turnip, peeled and diced
1 onion, skinned and chopped
2 sticks of celery, washed and chopped
1·25 ml (¼ level tsp) dried mixed herbs
900 ml (1½ pints) beef stock
15 ml (1 level tbsp) tomato paste
salt and freshly ground pepper
15 ml (1 level tbsp) cornflour
15 ml (1 tbsp) sherry

Skin the kidneys, cut in half and remove the cores. Cut into small pieces. Melt the butter in a saucepan and cook the vegetables for 10 minutes, until golden brown. Add the kidneys and cook for a further 2 minutes. Stir in the herbs, stock and tomato paste and season well. Bring to the boil and pour into the electric casserole. Place the lid in position and cook on high for 2½–3 hours or low for 5–6 hours.

Just before serving blend the cornflour to a smooth paste with a little water and stir into the soup with the sherry.

MAKES ABOUT 900 ML (1½ PINTS)

German potato soup

A hearty soup to serve as a winter snack

700 g (1½ lb) potatoes, peeled
75 g (3 oz) carrots, peeled
1 stick of celery, washed
1 leek, washed
100 g (4 oz) onion
100 g (4 oz) smoked bacon, rinded and diced
1·1 litres (2 pints) beef stock
5 ml (1 level tsp) salt
freshly ground black pepper
2·5 ml (½ level tsp) dried marjoram
2·5 ml (½ level tsp) dried mixed herbs
1 sprig parsley, with stem
100 g (4 oz) German sausage, chopped
5 ml (1 tsp) chopped parsley and croûtons to garnish

Cut the vegetables into small dice or slices. In a saucepan, fry the bacon until the fat runs. Add the vegetables and fry for 2–3 minutes. Add the stock, seasoning, herbs and German sausage. Bring to the boil and pour into the electric casserole. Stir well. Place the lid in position and cook on high for 3–4 hours or low for 6–8 hours. Serve garnished with chopped parsley and croûtons.

MAKES ABOUT 1·7 LITRES (3 PINTS)

Pot luck suppers

Step by step to cooking a basic brown stew in your electric casserole

1–2 onions, skinned and chopped
225 g (8 oz) root vegetables, carrot, swedes, parsnips, turnips, potatoes etc
700 g (1½ lb) stewing steak
salt and freshly ground pepper
25 g (1 oz) flour
15 ml (1 tbsp) oil or 25 g (1 oz) dripping or lard
400 ml (¾ pint) beef stock
5 ml (1 level tsp) dried mixed herbs (optional)
15 ml (1 level tbsp) tomato paste (optional)
15 ml (1 level tbsp) cornflour (if necessary)

1 Prepare the vegetables, cutting all root vegetables into 1-cm (½-in) pieces.

2 Trim the meat and cut into 5-cm (1-in) cubes. Toss in seasoned flour until evenly coated.

3 Heat the oil or fat in a frying pan, add the vegetables and cook for 5–10 minutes until softened and golden brown. Remove from the pan and place in the electric casserole packing them around the side and base.

4 Add the meat to the pan and cook for 5 minutes until browned on all sides. Place in the electric casserole in the 'well' of vegetables.

5 Stir the stock, herbs and tomato paste into the pan. Season well. Bring to the boil and pour into the electric casserole making sure that no meat residue is left in the pan.

6 Place the lid on the electric casserole and cook on HIGH for 3–4 hours or LOW for 6–8 hours according to your day's routine.

7 Thicken the juices, if necessary, with the cornflour blended with a little cold water. Stir into the casserole, replace the lid and continue cooking until the gravy is thickened.

Casseroled marrow slices

This is the easiest way to prepare marrow for the electric casserole

1 marrow, about 700–900 g (1½–2 lb)
15 ml (1 tbsp) vegetable oil
1 medium-sized onion, skinned and chopped
325 g (12 oz) minced beef
15 ml (1 level tbsp) tomato paste
15 ml (1 level tbsp) sweet chutney
2·5 ml (½ level tsp) curry paste
25 g (1 oz) sultanas
1·25 ml (¼ level tsp) salt
freshly ground black pepper

Cut the ends off the marrow, cut the marrow into four rings and peel thinly. Remove the seeds from the centre of each slice and stand each on a piece of foil large enough to seal completely.

Heat the oil in a frying pan and fry the onion for 5 minutes until soft. Add the mince and fry for 10 minutes until browned. Stir in the remaining ingredients. Divide the mince mixture into four and stuff into the centre of the marrow slices. Seal each parcel and place in the electric casserole with 150 ml (¼ pint) water. Place the lid in position and cook on high for 2–3 hours or low for 6–8 hours.

Bacon and fennel pot

50 g (2 oz) butter or margarine
325 g (12 oz) streaky bacon, rinded and coarsely chopped
900 g (2 lb) potatoes, peeled and thinly sliced
1 head of fennel, about 325 g (12 oz), trimmed and chopped
300 ml (½ pint) hot chicken stock
salt and freshly ground black pepper
142-ml (5-fl oz) carton soured cream

Melt the fat in a large frying pan. Fry the bacon for 5 minutes, add the potato slices and the fennel and fry for 5 minutes until the potatoes are golden. Transfer to the electric casserole, add the hot stock and the seasoning. Place the lid in position and cook on high for 2–3 hours or low for 4–6 hours. Just before serving stir in the soured cream.

Sausage stuffed courgettes

4 large courgettes
15 ml (1 tbsp) vegetable oil
225 g (8 oz) pork sausagemeat
1 small onion, skinned and chopped
45 ml (3 level tbsp) fresh white breadcrumbs
5 ml (1 tsp) Worcestershire sauce
15 ml (1 level tbsp) mango chutney
salt and freshly ground pepper
50 g (2 oz) Cheddar cheese, grated
75 ml (5 tbsp) chicken stock
5 ml (1 level tsp) cornflour

Cut a thin slice lengthways from each courgette and then cut in half to fit into the electric casserole. Scoop out the flesh in the centre of each courgette and chop. Heat the oil in a saucepan and fry the sausagemeat, chopped courgette and onion for 8–10 minutes until golden brown. Stir in the breadcrumbs, Worcestershire sauce, chutney and seasoning and cook for a further 2 minutes. Spoon into the courgette shells and sprinkle with grated cheese. Place the courgettes in the electric casserole and pour the stock around them. Place the lid in position and cook on high for 3–4 hours or low for 6–8 hours.

15 minutes before the end of cooking time remove the courgettes from the electric casserole and keep warm. Blend the cornflour to a smooth paste with a little water and stir into the juices in the casserole. Stir until the sauce thickens and pour over the courgette shells.

Lamb stuffed cabbage leaves

Lamb stuffed cabbage leaves

This is delicious served with plain boiled rice

700 g (1 ½ lb) firm green cabbage
15 ml (1 tbsp) vegetable oil
1 medium-sized onion, skinned and chopped
450 g (1 lb) boned shoulder of lamb, minced
60 ml (4 level tbsp) chutney
75 g (3 oz) raisins
5 ml (1 level tsp) salt
396-g (14-oz) can tomatoes
1 beef stock cube
15 ml (1 tbsp) Worcestershire sauce
pinch of paprika

Separate eight to ten large, but not outside leaves, from the cabbage and cut out the hard stem from the base of each. Wash in cold water then blanch in boiling water for 2 minutes; drain. Cut out the hard stem from the remaining leaves and shred finely.

Heat the oil in a frying pan and cook the onion and shredded cabbage for 2 minutes. Add the lamb and cook for 5–10 minutes until brown. Remove the pan from the heat and stir in the chutney, raisins and salt. Divide the mixture between the blanched leaves and fold each into a neat parcel and place in the greased electric casserole.

Purée the tomatoes in a blender or rub them through a sieve, then add the crumbled stock cube, Worcestershire sauce and paprika. Stir until well blended. Pour the tomato mixture over the cabbage leaves. Place the lid in position and cook on high for 3–4 hours or low for 6–8 hours.

Golden baked onions with tomato sauce

4 medium-sized onions, skinned
15 ml (1 tbsp) vegetable oil
100 g (4 oz) streaky bacon, rinded and chopped
10 ml (2 tsp) freshly chopped herbs
30 ml (2 level tbsp) fresh white breadcrumbs
15 ml (1 level tbsp) tomato paste
50 g (2 oz) Double Gloucester cheese, grated
salt and freshly ground pepper
25 g (1 oz) butter

For the sauce

15 g (½ oz) butter
1 clove of garlic, skinned and crushed
30 ml (2 level tbsp) flour
425-g (15-oz) can tomatoes
30 ml (2 level tbsp) tomato paste
150 ml (¼ pint) chicken stock
salt and freshly ground pepper
100 g (4 oz) button mushrooms, sliced

Cook the onions in boiling salted water for 15 minutes. Drain and remove the centre of each onion with a sharp knife. Heat the oil in a frying pan and fry the bacon for 10 minutes until crisp. Stir in the remaining ingredients except the butter and spoon into the cavity in each onion. Place a knob of butter on top of each onion and place in the electric casserole.

To make the sauce: melt the butter and fry the garlic in it for 1 minute. Add the remaining ingredients and bring to the boil, stirring. Pour the sauce into the electric casserole around the onions.

Place the lid in position and cook on high for 3–4 hours or low for 6–8 hours.

Stuffed aubergines

Check that the aubergines will fit into your electric casserole before starting

2 medium-sized aubergines, trimmed
15 ml (1 tbsp) vegetable oil
100 g (4 oz) minced beef
1 onion, skinned and finely chopped
1 clove of garlic, skinned and crushed
50 g (2 oz) flat mushrooms, finely chopped
50 g (2 oz) fresh white breadcrumbs
60 ml (4 level tbsp) tomato paste
2.5 ml (½ level tsp) dried mixed herbs
salt and freshly ground pepper
45 ml (3 tbsp) sherry or red wine
300 ml (½ pint) chicken stock
15 ml (1 level tbsp) cornflour

Cut the aubergines in half lengthways, scoop out the flesh and chop it very finely. Heat the oil in a frying pan, add the beef and fry for 5 minutes. Add the aubergines, onion, garlic and mushrooms and fry gently for a further 3–4 minutes. Add the breadcrumbs, half the tomato paste, the herbs and seasoning. Stir in the sherry and 30 ml (2 tbsp) water. Spoon the mixture into the aubergine halves and place in the electric casserole. Stir the remaining tomato paste and chicken stock together and pour around the aubergines. Place the lid in position and cook on high for 2½–3 hours or low for 5–6 hours.

15 minutes before the end of cooking time blend the cornflour to a smooth paste with a little water. Stir into the stock, replace the lid and continue cooking.

Golden baked onions with tomato sauce

✤ Onion and bacon hot pot

Red Leicester cheese has a particularly good flavour for this recipe but Cheddar cheese may also be used

30 ml (2 tbsp) vegetable oil
900 g (2 lb) small onions, skinned
325 g (12 oz) streaky bacon, rinded and chopped
30 ml (2 level tbsp) flour
300 ml (½ pint) beef stock
15 ml (1 level tbsp) tomato paste
185-g (6½-oz) can tomatoes
50 g (2 oz) seedless raisins
15 ml (1 tbsp) freshly chopped chives
pinch of sugar
50 g (2 oz) Red Leicester cheese, grated

Heat the oil in a large saucepan and fry the whole onions and the bacon for 10 minutes until golden brown. Stir in the flour and the remaining ingredients except the cheese and bring to the boil. Remove from the heat and stir in the cheese. Pour into the electric casserole and place the lid in position. Cook on high for 3–4 hours or low for 6–8 hours.

Freeze this recipe without the cheese—stir in the cheese when reheating

✤ Vegetable and bacon casserole

ILLUSTRATED IN COLOUR FACING PAGE 49

Either slice the cooked bacon joint or cut it into large chunks; serve with the vegetables to make an exciting and colourful meal

15 ml (1 tbsp) vegetable oil
450 g (1 lb) hock bacon joint, rinded
1 large onion, skinned and sliced
1 green pepper, seeded and sliced
2 large carrots, peeled and sliced
225 g (8 oz) potatoes, peeled and sliced
225 g (8 oz) button mushrooms
450 g (1 lb) tomatoes, skinned and sliced
30 ml (2 level tbsp) flour
900 ml (1½ pints) chicken or ham stock
1 bayleaf
salt and freshly ground pepper
15 ml (1 level tbsp) cornflour

Heat the oil in a large saucepan and fry the joint for 10 minutes until lightly browned on all sides. Remove from the pan and reserve. Add the onion, green pepper, carrots and potatoes and cook for 5–10 minutes until browned. Add the mushrooms and tomatoes and cook for a further 2 minutes. Place in the electric casserole. Stir the flour into the remaining fat in the pan, gradually add the stock and bring to the boil. Stir in the bayleaf and seasoning. Place the meat on top of the vegetables in the electric casserole and pour the liquid over it. Place the lid in position and cook on high for 4–5 hours or low for 8–10 hours.

15 minutes before the end of cooking time blend the cornflour to a smooth paste with a little water. Stir into the casserole, replace the lid and continue cooking.

Lasagne

If you have a removable earthenware casserole, pop it under a hot grill at the end of the cooking time to make a crisp golden top

25 g (1 oz) butter or margarine
1 large onion, skinned and chopped
1 clove of garlic, skinned and crushed
450 g (1 lb) lean minced beef
30 ml (2 level tbsp) tomato paste
5 ml (1 level tsp) salt
freshly ground pepper
150 ml (¼ pint) dry red wine
10 ml (2 level tsp) dried marjoram
225 g (8 oz) lasagne
25 g (1 oz) Parmesan cheese, grated

For the sauce
50 g (2 oz) butter
50 g (2 oz) flour
568 ml (1 pint) milk
salt and freshly ground pepper

Melt the fat in a saucepan and fry the onion and garlic for 5 minutes until soft. Stir in the mince and cook for 5 minutes. Stir in the tomato paste, seasoning, wine and marjoram. Bring to the boil, stirring.

To make the sauce: melt the butter in a saucepan, stir in the flour and cook for 1 minute. Gradually stir in the milk, season well. Bring to the boil, stirring all the time. Arrange the mince, lasagne and white sauce in layers in the electric casserole, finishing with sauce. Sprinkle with cheese. Place the lid in position and cook on high for 2–3 hours or low for 4–6 hours.

✤ Spaghetti bolognese

15 g (½ oz) butter or margarine
1 large onion, skinned and chopped
1 clove of garlic, skinned and crushed
450 g (1 lb) lean minced beef
396-g (14-oz) can tomatoes
300 ml (½ pint) beef stock
5 ml (1 level tsp) dried marjoram
7·5 ml (1½ level tsp) salt
freshly ground black pepper
100 g (4 oz) spaghetti broken into 7·5-cm (3-in) pieces
grated Parmesan cheese to garnish

Melt the fat in a frying pan and fry the onion and garlic for 5 minutes until soft. Add the mince and fry for 10 minutes until browned. Stir in the tomatoes, stock and seasonings. Bring to the boil and transfer to the electric casserole. Place the lid in position and cook on high for 2–3 hours or low for 4–6 hours.

45 minutes before the end of the cooking time turn the casserole to high, quickly stir in the broken spaghetti, replace the lid and continue cooking. Serve sprinkled with Parmesan cheese.
Freeze the sauce only

Cannelloni

A nutritious liver and spinach stuffed cannelloni supper dish. Serve it with a crisp green salad

12 cannelloni
396-g (14-oz) can tomatoes
300 ml (½ pint) chicken stock

For the stuffing
25 g (1 oz) butter
1 medium-sized onion, skinned and chopped
225 g (8 oz) lambs' liver
226-g (8-oz) packet frozen chopped spinach
40 g (1½ oz) fresh white breadcrumbs
pinch of ground nutmeg
salt and freshly ground pepper

To make the stuffing: melt the butter in a saucepan and fry the onion for 5 minutes. Trim the liver, chop it finely, add to the pan and fry for 5 minutes. Stir in the spinach, breadcrumbs, nutmeg and seasoning. Spoon the stuffing into the cannelloni and place in the electric casserole. Pour over the tomatoes and stock. Place the lid in position and cook on low for 2–2½ hours.

✤ Pepperpot supper

Use the smaller variety of pasta shells for this recipe or break spaghetti into 2·5-cm (1-in) lengths

450 g (1 lb) shin or skirt of beef
45 ml (3 tbsp) Worcestershire sauce
25 g (1 oz) butter or margarine
2 large onions, skinned and sliced
2 carrots, peeled and sliced
3 sticks of celery, washed and sliced
45 ml (3 level tbsp) flour
1·4 litres (2½ pints) beef stock
30 ml (2 level tbsp) tomato paste
10 ml (2 level tsp) salt
bouquet garni
50 g (2 oz) small pasta shapes

Pepperpot supper

Cut the beef into 2·5-cm (1-in) cubes. Place in a bowl with the Worcestershire sauce and marinate in the refrigerator for 2 hours or overnight.

Melt the fat in a large saucepan and fry the onions, carrots and celery for 5 minutes. Remove the meat from the marinade (reserving the marinade), add to the pan and fry for 10 minutes until browned. Stir in the flour and cook for 2 minutes. Gradually stir in the stock and the reserved marinade with the tomato paste, seasoning and bouquet garni and bring to the boil, stirring. Transfer to the electric casserole. Place the lid in position and cook on high for 4–5 hours or low for 8–10 hours or overnight.

45 minutes before the end of cooking time turn the casserole to high, stir in the pasta shapes, replace the lid and continue cooking.

Freeze without the pasta

Sausages with barbecue sauce

Just the thing for a teenagers' supper party

25 g (1 oz) butter or margarine
1 large onion, skinned and chopped
450 g (1 lb) pork sausages
226-g (8-oz) can tomatoes
10 ml (2 level tsp) tomato paste
30 ml (2 tbsp) vinegar
30 ml (2 level tbsp) demerara sugar
10 ml (2 level tsp) dry mustard
30 ml (2 tbsp) Worcestershire sauce
150 ml (¼ pint) beef stock
freshly ground black pepper
175 g (6 oz) pasta shapes

Melt the fat in a frying pan, add the onion and cook for 5 minutes until soft. Remove the onion from the pan and reserve; add the sausages and fry for 10 minutes until browned. Remove the sausages from the pan and drain off any surplus fat. Return the onion and sausages to the pan with the remaining ingredients, except the pasta. Bring to the boil, stirring, then transfer to the electric casserole. Place the lid in position and cook on high for 3–4 hours or low for 6–8 hours.

45 minutes before the end of cooking time turn the casserole to high. Stir in the pasta shapes, replace the lid and continue cooking.

Spiced minced lamb with pasta shells

45 ml (3 tbsp) vegetable oil
1 large onion, skinned and sliced
1 clove of garlic, skinned and crushed
450 g (1 lb) minced lamb
5 ml (1 level tsp) ground coriander
5 ml (1 level tsp) ground ginger
2·5 ml (½ level tsp) ground cummin
15 ml (1 level tbsp) plain flour
two 141-g (5-oz) cartons natural yogurt
185-g (6½-oz) can tomatoes
1 small green pepper, seeded and chopped
salt and freshly ground pepper
75 g (3 oz) pasta shells

Heat the oil in a saucepan and fry the onion and garlic for 5 minutes. Add the minced lamb and cook for a further 5 minutes. Stir in the spices and flour and cook for 1 minute. Stir in the yogurt, tomatoes, green pepper and seasoning. Pour into the electric casserole and place the lid in position. Cook on high for 2–3 hours or low for 4–6 hours.

45 minutes before the end of cooking time turn the electric casserole to high, stir in the pasta shells and continue cooking.

Pork with beans and orange

225 g (8 oz) red kidney beans, soaked overnight
30 ml (2 tbsp) vegetable oil
325 g (12 oz) streaky salt pork, trimmed and diced
1 large onion, skinned and sliced
45 ml (3 level tbsp) flour
225 g (8 oz) carrots, peeled and sliced
400 ml (¾ pint) chicken stock
1 bayleaf
salt and freshly ground pepper
1 orange

Soak the kidney beans overnight and drain. Heat the oil in a saucepan and cook the pork for 10 minutes until golden brown. Add the onion and cook for 3 minutes. Stir in the flour and cook for 1 minute. Add the carrots, stock, bayleaf and seasoning. Peel two or three pieces of rind from the orange and add to the pan with 60 ml (4 tbsp) orange juice and the beans. Bring to the boil, stirring. Pour into the electric casserole, place the lid in position and cook on high for 3–4 hours or low for 6–8 hours.

Bean and aubergine curry

225 g (8 oz) red kidney beans, soaked overnight
450 g (1 lb) aubergines, trimmed and sliced
salt
25 g (1 oz) butter
2 medium-sized onions, skinned and sliced
100 g (4 oz) streaky bacon, rinded and chopped
2·5 ml (½ level tsp) each of ground ginger,
    turmeric, coriander
30 ml (2 level tbsp) curry paste
15 ml (1 level tbsp) flour
300 ml (½ pint) beef stock

Soak the kidney beans overnight and drain. Sprinkle the aubergines with salt. Leave them to stand for 20 minutes then wash in cold water and dry with kitchen paper towel. Melt the butter in a saucepan and sauté the onion for 5 minutes until soft. Add the bacon and cook for 2–3 minutes. Stir in the spices and flour and cook for 1 minute. Gradually add the stock and bring to the boil, stirring. Add the beans and aubergines and place in the electric casserole. Place the lid in position and cook on high for 2–3 hours or low for 4–6 hours.

Chicken and mushroom risotto

450 g (1 lb) cooked chicken
25 g (1 oz) butter
2 medium-sized onions, skinned and chopped
3 sticks of celery, washed and chopped
1 small green pepper, seeded and chopped
100 g (4 oz) streaky bacon, rinded and chopped
225 g (8 oz) long grain rice
900 ml (1½ pints) chicken stock
salt and freshly ground pepper
100 g (4 oz) button mushrooms
2 large tomatoes, skinned and quartered
2·5 ml (½ level tsp) dried basil

Chop the chicken into fairly large pieces. Melt

the butter in a large saucepan and fry the onion, celery, green pepper and bacon for 10 minutes until the bacon has browned. Stir in the rice and add the stock, seasoning, mushrooms, tomatoes, basil and the chicken and bring to the boil. Pour into the electric casserole and place the lid in position. Cook on high for 2–3 hours or low for 4–6 hours.

Cider sausage pot

Serve with crusty French bread or granary rolls

700 g (1½ lb) pork sausages
25 g (1 oz) butter or margarine
225 g (8 oz) leeks, washed and sliced
450 g (1 lb) cooking apples, peeled, cored and
    sliced
57-g (2¼-oz) packet instant potato
salt and freshly ground black pepper
225 ml (8 fl oz) dry cider

Cut each sausage into four pieces. Melt the fat in a frying pan and cook the sausages and leeks for 10 minutes until browned. Cook the apples in boiling water for 1 minute; drain well. Place the sausage mixture and apples in the electric casserole. Sprinkle the instant potato and seasoning on top, pour over the cider and stir well. Place the lid in position and cook on high for 2–3 hours or low for 4–6 hours.

Frankfurter supper pot

1 green pepper, seeded
100 g (4 oz) button mushrooms
1 small cauliflower
25 g (1 oz) butter or margarine
100 g (4 oz) pasta shells
396-g (14-oz) can tomatoes
150 ml (¼ pint) beef stock
210-g (7-oz) packet frankfurters
5 ml (1 level tsp) salt
freshly ground black pepper
75 g (3 oz) Cheddar cheese, grated

Thinly slice the pepper, cut the mushrooms in half and divide the cauliflower into florets. Grease the electric casserole with the fat and arrange the vegetables, pasta shells and frankfurters in layers. Pour over the stock and any juice from the tomatoes. Season well and top with cheese. Place the lid in position and cook on high for 2–3 hours or low for 4–6 hours.

Lamb and apple risotto

Delicious on its own or served with crisp cooked broccoli

25 g (1 oz) butter
450 g (1 lb) best end neck or loin of lamb, trimmed and cubed
1 small onion, skinned and chopped
2 sticks of celery, washed and chopped
2 large cooking apples, peeled, cored and chopped
225 g (8 oz) long grain rice
5 ml (1 level tsp) dry mustard
rind and juice of ½ lemon
50 g (2 oz) seedless raisins
600 ml (1 pint) chicken stock
300 ml (½ pint) dry cider
salt and freshly ground pepper

Melt the butter in a large saucepan and fry the meat and onion for 5–10 minutes until golden brown. Add the celery, apples and rice and cook for a further two minutes. Stir in the remaining ingredients and pour into the electric casserole. Place the lid in position and cook on high for 2–3 hours or low for 4–6 hours.

✤ Butter bean and vegetable stew

ILLUSTRATED IN COLOUR FACING PAGE 49

Cider gives a distinctive, fruity flavour to this colourful vegetable stew

175 g (6 oz) butter beans, soaked overnight
25 g (1 oz) butter
225 g (8 oz) courgettes, trimmed and sliced
225 g (8 oz) aubergines, trimmed and sliced
3 sticks of celery, trimmed and chopped
1 medium-sized red pepper, seeded and chopped
150 ml (¼ pint) dry cider
700 ml (1¼ pints) chicken stock
2·5 ml (½ level tsp) dried thyme
salt and freshly ground pepper
30 ml (2 level tbsp) cornflour
freshly chopped parsley to garnish

Soak the butter beans overnight and drain. Melt the butter in a saucepan, add the vegetables and cook for 10 minutes until golden brown. Stir in the beans, cider, stock, thyme and seasoning. Bring to the boil and pour into the electric casserole. Place the lid in position and cook on high for 3–4 hours or low for 6–8 hours.

15 minutes before the end of cooking time blend the cornflour to a smooth paste with a little water. Stir into the casserole, replace the lid and continue cooking. Serve garnished with parsley.

Chicken and bacon balls in tomato sauce

Serve with boiled rice or buttered noodles for a really filling family meal

450 g (1 lb) chicken meat
225 g (8 oz) streaky bacon, rinded
1 small onion, skinned
175 g (6 oz) fresh white breadcrumbs
salt and freshly ground pepper
5 ml (1 level tsp) ground nutmeg
15 ml (1 level tbsp) tomato paste
142-ml (5-fl oz) carton soured cream
1 egg, beaten
30 ml (2 tbsp) vegetable oil

For the sauce
15 ml (1 tbsp) vegetable oil
450 g (1 lb) tomatoes, skinned and chopped
1 large onion, skinned and chopped
1 clove of garlic, skinned and crushed
30 ml (2 level tbsp) flour
30 ml (2 level tbsp) tomato paste
600 ml (1 pint) chicken stock
salt and freshly ground pepper

Mince the chicken, bacon and onion together. Add all the remaining ingredients except the oil and stir until well combined. Shape the meat mixture into balls the size of a walnut. Heat the oil in a frying pan and fry the meat balls for 4–5 minutes until golden brown. Drain on kitchen paper towel.

To make the sauce: heat the oil in a saucepan and fry the tomatoes, onion and garlic for 2–3 minutes. Add the flour and tomato paste and cook for a further minute. Gradually add the stock and seasoning and bring to the boil.

Pour the sauce into the electric casserole and add the meat balls. Stir to coat the meat balls with sauce. Place the lid in position and cook on high for 2–3 hours or low for 4–6 hours.

✢ Liver and bacon casserole

450 g (1 lb) lambs' liver
salt and freshly ground pepper
25 g (1 oz) flour
15 ml (1 tbsp) vegetable oil
2 medium-sized onions, skinned and chopped
4 rashers back bacon, rinded and chopped
100 g (4 oz) mushrooms
300 ml (½ pint) beef stock
15 ml (1 level tbsp) tomato paste

Wash and dry the liver and cut into thin slices. Toss in seasoned flour. Heat the oil in a frying pan, fry the liver for 5 minutes and place in the electric casserole. Add the onions and bacon to the pan, fry for 5 minutes and place in the electric casserole. Add the remaining in-

gredients to the pan and bring to the boil. Pour over the liver in the electric casserole and stir well. Place the lid in position and cook on high for 2–3 hours or low for 4–6 hours.

✢ Lamb curry

Serve this traditional dish with plain boiled rice and poppadums

50 g (2 oz) butter or margarine
2 medium-sized onions, skinned and sliced
1 clove of garlic, skinned and crushed
2 sticks of celery, washed and sliced
700 g (1½ lb) boned shoulder of lamb, trimmed and cut into 2·5-cm (1-in) cubes
30 ml (2 level tbsp) curry powder
30 ml (2 level tbsp) flour
300 ml (½ pint) beef stock
30 ml (2 level tbsp) chutney
1 large banana
141-g (5-oz) carton natural yogurt

Heat the fat in a large frying pan and fry the

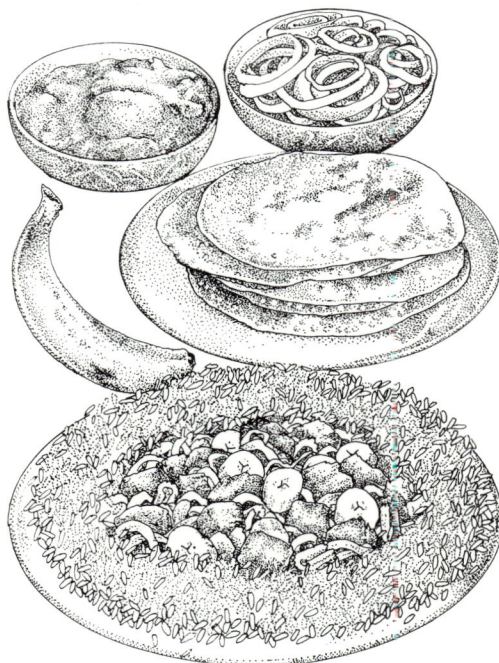

Lamb curry

vegetables for 5 minutes until soft. Add the meat and fry for 10 minutes until browned. Stir in the curry powder and flour and cook for 2 minutes. Gradually add the stock and chutney; bring to the boil, stirring. Transfer to the electric casserole. Place the lid in position and cook on high for 3–4 hours or low for 6–8 hours.

20 minutes before the end of cooking time turn the electric casserole to high. Chop the banana and add to the electric casserole with the yogurt. Replace the lid and continue cooking.

Freeze without the banana and yogurt

Sausage and corn medley

Sausage cakes cooked with a colourful selection of vegetables

225 g (8 oz) spiral macaroni
15 ml (1 tbsp) vegetable oil
1 large onion, skinned and chopped
1 large green pepper, seeded and sliced
450 g (1 lb) sausagemeat
30 ml (2 level tbsp) flour
568 ml (1 pint) milk
60 ml (4 level tbsp) tomato paste
salt and freshly ground pepper
326-g (11 ½-oz) can sweetcorn
2 large tomatoes, skinned and sliced
parsley sprigs to garnish

Cook the macaroni in boiling salted water for 5 minutes, drain and reserve. Heat the oil in a frying pan and cook the onion and pepper for 5 minutes until soft. Drain and transfer to the electric casserole. Shape the sausagemeat into twelve small cakes with floured hands. Add to the pan and cook for 10 minutes until golden brown on both sides. Drain and transfer to the electric casserole. Stir the flour into the pan juices and cook for 1 minute. Gradually add the milk and bring to the boil, stirring. Cook for 1–2 minutes, then stir in the tomato paste, seasoning, sweetcorn and cooked macaroni. Pour over the sausage cakes in the electric casserole and stir well. Arrange the tomato slices on top. Place the lid in position and cook on high 3–4 hours or low 6–8 hours. Serve garnished with parsley sprigs.

✤ Turkey and tomato casserole

325 g (12 oz) turkey breast
15 ml (1 tbsp) vegetable oil
1 large onion, skinned and sliced
100 g (4 oz) streaky bacon, rinded and chopped
225 g (8 oz) tomatoes, skinned and quartered
225 g (8 oz) button mushrooms
salt and freshly ground pepper
15 ml (1 tbsp) freshly chopped chives
600 ml (1 pint) chicken stock
45 ml (3 tbsp) sherry
30 ml (2 level tbsp) tomato paste
45 ml (3 level tbsp) plain flour
225 g (8 oz) pasta shells

Cut the turkey breast into 1-cm (½-in) cubes. Heat the oil in a frying pan and cook the onion and bacon for 5 minutes. Add the turkey, tomatoes and mushrooms and cook for 5 minutes. Stir in the seasoning, chives and stock. Blend the sherry, tomato paste and flour together and add to the turkey mixture. Bring to the boil and pour into the electric casserole. Place the lid in position and cook on high for 3–4 hours or low for 6–8 hours.

30 minutes before the end of cooking time turn the electric casserole to high, stir in the pasta shells and continue cooking.

Freeze without the pasta

✤ Spiced turkey supper

about 325 g (12 oz) turkey flesh, from 3 large drumsticks
25 g (1 oz) flour
salt and freshly ground pepper
15 ml (1 tbsp) vegetable oil
25 g (1 oz) butter
1 medium-sized onion, skinned and chopped
1 small green pepper, seeded and thinly sliced
1 clove of garlic, skinned and crushed
15 ml (1 level tbsp) flour
300 ml (½ pint) chicken stock
100 g (4 oz) button mushrooms, thinly sliced
7·5 ml (1 ½ level tsp) curry powder
5 ml (1 level tsp) ground mace
1 large cooking apple, peeled, cored and thinly sliced
15 ml (1 level tbsp) sweet chutney
15 ml (1 tbsp) lemon juice

Cut the turkey flesh from the joints into large pieces and coat in seasoned flour. Heat the oil and butter in a frying pan and cook the onion, pepper and garlic for 5 minutes until soft. Remove from the pan and place in the electric casserole. Add the turkey to the pan and cook for 5 minutes, until golden brown. Place in the electric casserole. Add the flour to the pan and cook for 1 minute. Gradually stir in the stock with all the other ingredients. Bring to the boil, pour over the turkey in the electric casserole and stir well. Place the lid in position and cook on high for 3–4 hours or low for 6–8 hours.

Veal and bacon pudding

You'll find this a good recipe for making a little meat go a long way.

For the filling
225 g (8 oz) boned fore-hock bacon joint
1·25–2·5 ml (¼–½ tsp) dried thyme
grated rind of ½ lemon
60 ml (4 level tbsp) flour
salt and freshly ground black pepper
325 g (12 oz) stewing veal, trimmed and diced
50 g (2 oz) button mushrooms, quartered
1 medium-sized onion, skinned and chopped
15 ml (1 level tbsp) tomato paste
150 ml (¼ pint) water

For the pastry
225 g (8 oz) self raising flour
pinch of salt
100 g (4 oz) shredded suet

To make the filling: trim the rind and excess fat from the bacon joint and dice. Stir the thyme, lemon rind, flour and seasoning together, add the bacon, veal and vegetables and stir until well coated with seasoned flour.

To make the pastry: stir the flour, salt and suet together. Add enough cold water to mix to a soft dough. Roll out and use two thirds of the pastry to line a greased 1·1-litre (2-pint) pudding basin. Spoon in the filling. Blend the tomato paste and water together and pour over the meat. Cover with the pastry lid and seal the edges well. Cover with greased greaseproof paper and foil and secure with string. Place in the electric casserole with boiling water to come halfway up the basin. Place the lid in position and cook on high for 4–6 hours.

Liver and bacon pudding

For the filling
15 g (½ oz) butter
225 g (8 oz) streaky bacon, rinded and chopped
1 large onion, skinned and chopped
450 g (1 lb) lambs' liver, washed and chopped
30 ml (2 level tbsp) flour
30 ml (2 level tbsp) tomato paste
75 ml (5 tbsp) chicken stock
salt and freshly ground pepper

For the pastry
225 g (8 oz) self raising flour
pinch of salt
100 g (4 oz) shredded suet

To make the filling: melt the butter in a frying pan and cook the bacon and onion for 5 minutes until brown. Add the liver and cook gently for 3–4 minutes. Stir in the other filling ingredients and bring to the boil.

To make the pastry: stir the flour, salt and suet together in a bowl. Add enough cold water to mix to a soft dough. Roll out and use two thirds of the pastry to line a 1·1-litre (2-pint) pudding basin. Spoon in the filling, cover with the pastry lid and seal the edges well. Cover with greased greaseproof paper and foil and secure with string. Place in the electric casserole with boiling water to come halfway up the basin. Place the lid in position and cook on high for 4–6 hours.

✥ Chilli con carne

275 g (10 oz) red kidney beans, soaked overnight
15 ml (1 tbsp) vegetable oil
1 large onion, skinned and chopped
700 g (1½ lb) minced beef
225 g (8 oz) tomatoes, skinned and chopped
30 ml (2 level tbsp) tomato paste
salt and freshly ground pepper
5–10 ml (1–2 level tsp) chilli powder
15 ml (1 tbsp) tomato chutney
1–2·5 ml (¼–½ tsp) Tabasco sauce
300 ml (½ pint) beef stock
15 ml (1 level tbsp) cornflour

Soak the kidney beans overnight and drain.

Heat the oil in a large saucepan and fry the onion for 2–3 minutes until softened. Add all the remaining ingredients except the cornflour and fry for 5 minutes.

Mix the cornflour to a smooth paste with a little water, stir into the pan and bring to the boil, stirring. Pour into the electric casserole and place the lid in position. Cook on high for 2–3 hours or low for 4–6 hours.

✢ Chicken and leek pudding

The electric casserole makes delicious, fluffy suet crust pastry

For the filling
3 chicken portions, skinned
225 g (8 oz) leeks, sliced and washed
100 g (4 oz) carrots, peeled and grated
45 ml (3 level tbsp) flour
finely grated rind of ½ lemon
salt and freshly ground pepper
150 ml (¼ pint) chicken stock

For the pastry
225 g (8 oz) self raising flour
pinch of salt
100 g (4 oz) shredded suet

To make the filling: cut the meat from the chicken portions and chop it coarsely. Stir the chicken and the remaining filling ingredients together.

To make the pastry: stir the flour, salt and suet together. Add enough cold water to mix to a soft dough. Roll out and use two thirds of the pastry to line a 1·1-litre (2-pint) pudding basin. Spoon in the filling, cover with the pastry lid and seal the edges well. Cover with greased greaseproof paper and foil and secure with string. Place in the electric casserole with boiling water to come halfway up the basin. Place the lid in position and cook on high for 4–6 hours.

✢ Liver stroganoff

450 g (1 lb) lambs' liver
salt and freshly ground pepper
30 ml (2 level tbsp) flour
50 g (2 oz) butter
1 onion, skinned and chopped
1 green pepper, seeded and sliced
225 g (8 oz) button mushrooms, sliced
600 ml (1 pint) beef stock
15 ml (1 level tbsp) tomato paste
2·5 ml (½ level tsp) dried mixed herbs
142-ml (5-fl oz) carton soured cream
freshly chopped parsley to garnish

Chicken and leek pudding

Slice the liver and cut into thin strips. Toss in seasoned flour. Melt the butter in a frying pan and cook the onion and pepper for 5 minutes, until soft. Add the mushrooms and liver and cook for 2–3 minutes. Stir in the stock, herbs and tomato paste and bring to the boil. Pour into the electric casserole and stir well. Place the lid in position and cook on high for 2–2½ hours or low for 4–5 hours.

Just before serving, stir in the soured cream and sprinkle with parsley.

Freeze without the soured cream

Moussaka

Traditionally, moussaka is made with lamb, but beef makes a good substitute

45 ml (3 tbsp) vegetable oil
2 aubergines, sliced
4 medium-sized onions, skinned and sliced
450 g (1 lb) minced lamb or beef
30 ml (2 level tbsp) flour
salt and freshly ground pepper
4 tomatoes, skinned and sliced
150 ml (¼ pint) beef stock
45 ml (3 level tbsp) tomato paste
2 eggs
141-g (5-oz) carton natural yogurt

Heat the oil in a frying pan and fry the aubergine slices for 5 minutes. Place half the aubergines in the base of the electric casserole. Add the onions to the pan and fry for 5 minutes. Add the meat and cook for 10 minutes until browned. Stir in the flour and cook for 1 minute. Season well. Spoon the meat over the aubergines in the electric casserole. Add the remaining aubergines and arrange the tomatoes on top. Stir the stock and tomato paste together and pour over the tomatoes. Place the lid in position and cook on high for 2–3 hours or low for 4–6 hours.

30 minutes before the end of cooking time turn the electric casserole to high. Beat the eggs and yogurt together, pour over the moussaka, replace the lid and continue cooking.

Kidney and sausage braise

6 lambs' kidneys
225 g (8 oz) sausagemeat
25 g (1 oz) butter or margarine
100 g (4 oz) streaky bacon, rinded and chopped
1 large onion, skinned and chopped
30 ml (2 level tbsp) tomato paste
30 ml (2 level tbsp) flour
600 ml (1 pint) beef stock
salt and freshly ground pepper
1 bayleaf
100 g (4 oz) pasta shells

Skin, halve and core the kidneys. Shape the sausagemeat into balls. Melt the fat in a frying pan and fry the kidneys, sausagemeat balls, bacon and onion for 10 minutes until browned. Add the tomato paste and flour, gradually stir in the stock, add the seasoning and bayleaf and bring to the boil. Pour into the electric casserole and place the lid in position. Cook on high for 3–4 hours or low for 6–8 hours.

45 minutes before the end of cooking time turn the electric casserole to high, stir in the pasta shells, replace the lid and continue cooking.

✤ Minced beef with red peppers

Everyday mince brightened up with red peppers, mushrooms and a little cream

25 g (1 oz) butter
1 medium-sized onion, skinned and chopped
2 red peppers, seeded and sliced
450 g (1 lb) minced beef
45 ml (3 level tbsp) flour
300 ml (½ pint) beef stock
225 g (8 oz) flat mushrooms, sliced
10 ml (2 tsp) Worcestershire sauce
15 ml (1 level tbsp) tomato paste
salt and freshly ground pepper
142-ml (5-fl oz) carton soured cream
freshly chopped parsley to garnish

Melt the butter in a frying pan and cook the

onion and peppers for 5 minutes. Add the meat and cook for 5 minutes until browned. Stir in the flour and cook for 1–2 minutes, stirring. Gradually stir in the stock with the mushrooms, Worcestershire sauce, tomato paste and seasoning. Bring to the boil before transferring to the electric casserole. Place the lid in position and cook on high for 2–3 hours or low for 4–6 hours.

Just before serving pour in the soured cream and stir once or twice, then sprinkle with parsley.

Freeze without the soured cream

✤ Spiced meat loaf with peanut topping

Serve hot with tomato sauce or cold with a mixed salad

75 g (3 oz) fresh white breadcrumbs
225 g (8 oz) liver sausage, finely diced
1 medium-sized onion, skinned and finely
   chopped
1 clove of garlic, skinned and crushed
225 g (8 oz) minced beef
1 carrot, peeled and grated
salt and freshly ground pepper
5 ml (1 level tsp) ground nutmeg
1 egg, beaten
30 ml (2 level tbsp) tomato paste
25 g (1 oz) peanuts, finely chopped

Grease a 450-g (1-lb) loaf tin and coat with 25 g (1 oz) breadcrumbs. In a large bowl mix all the ingredients together except the peanuts. Press the mixture into the prepared tin and smooth the top with a spoon. Cover tightly with a double layer of foil. Place in the electric casserole with enough boiling water to come half-way up the sides of the tin. Place the lid in position and cook on high for 3–4 hours or low for 6–8 hours. Turn on to a heated serving dish and press the chopped peanuts into the top of the loaf.

Freeze without the peanut topping

Creamed haddock bake

Don't cook this longer than suggested as the fish will start to toughen

25 g (1 oz) butter
15 ml (1 tbsp) vegetable oil
1 medium-sized onion, skinned and chopped
450 g (1 lb) potatoes, peeled and cubed
45 ml (3 level tbsp) flour
150 ml (¼ pint) chicken stock
300 ml (½ pint) milk
45 ml (3 tbsp) cream or top of the milk
5 ml (1 level tsp) capers, finely chopped
2·5 ml (½ level tsp) salt
paprika pepper
198-g (7-oz) can sweetcorn kernels
450 g (1 lb) smoked haddock, skinned, boned and
   flaked

Heat the butter and oil in a large saucepan and fry the onion and potatoes for 10 minutes until golden brown. Remove from the pan and place in the electric casserole. Stir the flour into the remaining fat in the pan, stir in the stock and milk and bring to the boil. Add the remaining ingredients and pour into the electric casserole. Stir well. Place the lid in position and cook on high for 2–3 hours or low for 4–6 hours.

Haddock chowder

A wholesome fish soup which makes a complete meal in itself

15 ml (1 tbsp) vegetable oil
1 medium-sized onion, skinned and sliced
3 rashers of streaky bacon, rinded and chopped
2 courgettes, washed and sliced
225 g (8 oz) potatoes, peeled and sliced
15 ml (1 level tbsp) flour
600 ml (1 pint) fish or chicken stock
salt and freshly ground pepper
450 g (1 lb) smoked haddock fillet
225 g (8 oz) tomatoes, skinned and quartered
1 bayleaf
bouquet garni
freshly chopped chives to garnish

Heat the oil in a large saucepan and fry the

onion and bacon for 5 minutes until soft. Add the courgettes and potatoes and fry for a further 3 minutes. Add the flour and gradually stir in the stock. Season and bring to the boil, stirring.

Cut the haddock into 5-cm (2-in) cubes and add to the pan with the remaining ingredients. Pour into the electric casserole and place the lid in position. Cook on high for 2–3 hours or low for 4–6 hours. Serve sprinkled with chopped chives.

Cheese tuna pudding

Flaked tuna fish and sweetcorn in a creamy sauce encased in fluffy suet crust pastry

For the pastry
175 g (6 oz) self raising flour
2·5 ml (½ level tsp) salt
freshly ground black pepper
2·5 ml (½ level tsp) dry mustard
75 g (3 oz) shredded suet
50 g (2 oz) Cheddar cheese, grated

For the filling
25 g (1 oz) butter or margarine
45 ml (3 level tbsp) flour
300 ml (½ pint) milk
198-g (7-oz) can tuna, drained and flaked
326-g (11½-oz) can sweetcorn kernels
5 ml (1 level tsp) salt
freshly ground black pepper

To make the pastry: sift the flour and seasonings together and stir in the suet and grated cheese. Mix with enough water to form a soft dough. Knead lightly on a floured surface. Use two thirds to line a greased 900-ml (1½-pint) pudding basin.

To make the filling: melt the fat in a saucepan, add the flour and cook for 1–2 minutes, stirring. Gradually stir in the milk, bring to the boil, stirring, and cook for 1–2 minutes. Add the tuna fish, sweetcorn and seasonings. Pour the filling into the basin and cover with the remaining pastry. Cover with greased greaseproof paper and foil and secure with string. Place in the electric casserole and pour in enough boiling water to come halfway up the basin. Place the lid in position and cook on high for 3 hours.

Family fare

✤ Lamb and apple casserole

Use a small sprig of fresh rosemary instead of dried for a slightly stronger flavour

1·1 kg (2½ lb) middle neck of lamb, boned
salt and freshly ground pepper
25 g (1 oz) flour
25 g (1 oz) butter
2 medium-sized onions, skinned and chopped
700 g (1½ lb) potatoes, peeled and sliced
1 large cooking apple, peeled, cored and sliced
300 ml (½ pint) beef stock
15 ml (1 tbsp) Worcestershire sauce
2·5 ml (½ level tsp) dried rosemary

Trim the meat and cut into 2-cm (¾-in) cubes. Toss in seasoned flour. Melt the butter in a frying pan, add the meat, cook for 10 minutes until browned and place in the electric casserole. Add the vegetables to the pan and cook for 5 minutes until golden brown. Stir in the apple, stock and Worcestershire sauce. Season, add the dried rosemary and bring to the boil, stirring. Pour into the electric casserole and stir well. Place the lid in position and cook on high for 3–4 hours or low for 6–8 hours.

Barbecued lamb

Long slow cooking ensures the lamb absorbs the beautiful flavour of this barbecue sauce

900 g (2 lb) breast of lamb
30 ml (2 tbsp) vegetable oil
1 medium-sized onion, skinned and sliced
1 clove of garlic, skinned and crushed
2·5 ml (½ level tsp) dry mustard
1·25 ml (¼ level tsp) ground ginger
1·25 ml (¼ level tsp) cayenne pepper
10 ml (2 level tsp) sugar
30 ml (2 level tbsp) tomato paste
30 ml (2 tbsp) Worcestershire sauce
15 ml (1 tbsp) vinegar
226-g (8-oz) can pineapple pieces

Trim any excess fat from the lamb and cut into pieces, between the ribs. Heat the oil in a frying pan and fry the meat for 10 minutes until browned. Drain and reserve. Add the onion and garlic to the frying pan and fry for about 5 minutes until soft. Add the seasoning, sugar, tomato paste, Worcestershire sauce, vinegar and the pineapple pieces with the juice. Bring to the boil, stirring. Transer to the electric casserole with the meat. Place the lid position and cook on high for 3–4 hours or low for 6–8 hours.

✤ Traditional hot pot

A true Lancashire hot pot also includes oysters

15 ml (1 tbsp) vegetable oil
8 middle neck lamb chops
2 large onions, skinned and sliced
2 large carrots, peeled and sliced
900 g (2 lb) potatoes, peeled and sliced
salt and freshly ground pepper
600 ml (1 pint) beef stock

Heat the oil in a frying pan and cook the chops for 3–4 minutes on both sides until browned. Remove from the pan and place in the electric casserole. Add the vegetables to the frying pan and sauté for 5–10 minutes until lightly browned. Season the vegetables, place in the electric casserole, arranging a layer of potato on the top. Pour over the stock. Place the lid in position and cook on high for 3–4 hours or low for 6–8 hours.

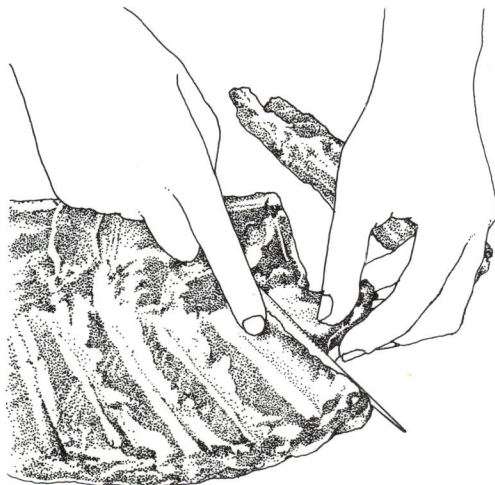

Cutting a breast of lamb into ribs for Barbecued lamb

✤ Blanquette of lamb with beans

225 g (8 oz) butter beans, soaked overnight
45 ml (3 tbsp) vegetable oil
450 g (1 lb) boned leg of lamb, cubed
225 g (8 oz) carrots, peeled and quartered
3 medium-sized onions, skinned and sliced
400 ml (¾ pint) beef stock
salt and freshly ground pepper
50 g (2 oz) butter or margarine
60 ml (4 level tbsp) flour
90 ml (6 tbsp) top of milk
45 ml (3 tbsp) freshly chopped parsley

Soak the butter beans overnight and drain. Heat the oil in a frying pan and cook the lamb for 5 minutes until browned. Place in the electric casserole. Add the carrots and onions to the pan and cook for 5 minutes. Place in the electric casserole with the stock, seasoning and beans. Place the lid in position and cook on high for 3–4 hours or low for 6–8 hours.

10 minutes before the end of cooking time melt the fat in a pan, stir in the flour and cook for 1 minute. Add the milk and bring to the boil. Stir into the electric casserole with the parsley and serve.

Spiced lamb with aubergines

This is a highly spiced recipe for curry lovers. If you prefer a milder taste, reduce the quantity of chilli seasoning and curry paste used. Serve with plain boiled rice

450 g (1 lb) aubergines, sliced
salt
1 kg (2¼ lb) lean breast of lamb, boned
25 g (1 oz) lard
1 large onion, skinned and chopped
5 ml (1 level tsp) ground turmeric
5 ml (1 level tsp) chilli seasoning
5 ml (1 level tsp) ground cummin
5 ml (1 level tsp) salt
30 ml (2 level tbsp) curry paste
45 ml (3 level tbsp) mango chutney
75 g (3 oz) sultanas
30 ml (2 level tbsp) peanut butter
15 ml (1 tbsp) Worcestershire sauce
300 ml (½ pint) beef stock

Sprinkle the aubergines liberally with salt and leave for about 30 minutes. Wash thoroughly and dry with kitchen paper towel. Trim any fat off the lamb and cut into 1-cm (½-in) cubes. Melt the lard in a frying pan and fry the aubergines for 5 minutes until soft. Remove from the pan and reserve. Add the onion and fry for 5 minutes. Add the meat and continue frying for 10 minutes until browned. Add the spices, the salt and curry paste and cook for 5 minutes, stirring. Stir in the remaining ingredients, bring to the boil and transfer to the electric casserole with the aubergines. Place the lid in position and cook on high for 3–4 hours or low for 6–8 hours.

✤ Lemon lamb meatballs in tomato sauce

Garnish with chopped parsley and serve with French bread

450 g (1 lb) minced lamb
75 g (3 oz) fresh white breadcrumbs
45 ml (3 level tbsp) horseradish sauce
7·5 ml (1½ level tsp) ground paprika
salt and freshly ground pepper
1 large egg
grated rind and juice of 1 lemon
45 ml (3 level tbsp) plain flour
45 ml (3 tbsp) vegetable oil
1 large onion, skinned and sliced
1 clove of garlic, skinned and crushed
185-g (6½-oz) can tomatoes
300 ml (½ pint) beef stock
chopped parsley

Stir the lamb, breadcrumbs, horseradish sauce, paprika, seasoning, egg, lemon rind and 15 ml (1 tbsp) lemon juice together until well mixed. Shape into sixteen small balls and coat in flour. Heat the oil in a frying pan and cook the meatballs for 8–10 minutes until well browned. Drain thoroughly on kitchen paper towel and place in the electric casserole.

Add the onion to the pan and cook for 10 minutes, until golden brown. Stir in any remaining flour with the garlic, tomatoes, stock, seasoning and 15 ml (1 tbsp) lemon juice. Bring to the boil and pour over the meatballs in the electric casserole. Place the lid in position and cook on high for 2–3 hours or low for 4–6 hours.

✣ Lemon layered lamb chops

Freshly chopped mint adds a summer flavour to this casserole

4 lamb chops
15 ml (1 tbsp) vegetable oil
4 slices of lemon
2 medium-sized onions, skinned and sliced
1 small green pepper, seeded and sliced
30 ml (2 level tbsp) flour
300 ml (½ pint) chicken stock
15 ml (1 tbsp) freshly chopped mint
salt and freshly ground pepper
freshly chopped mint to garnish

Trim excess fat from the chops. Heat the oil in a frying pan and cook the chops for 5 minutes each side until lightly browned. Drain on kitchen paper towel and place in the electric casserole with a lemon slice on each chop. Add the onions and pepper to the pan and cook for 5 minutes until soft. Spoon the onion and pepper over the chops. Blend the flour with the remaining oil in the pan and stir in the stock. Bring to the boil, stirring continuously. Add the mint and seaon to taste. Pour the sauce over the chops. Place the lid in position and cook on high for 3–4 hours or low for 6–8 hours. Serve garnished with fresh mint.

✣ Lamb and tomato casserole

Vegetables add flavour and colour to lamb cutlets

8 lamb cutlets
30 ml (2 tbsp) vegetable oil
2 medium-sized onions, skinned and chopped
2 sticks of celery, washed and chopped
225 g (8 oz) mushrooms, sliced
450 g (1 lb) tomatoes, skinned and quartered
30 ml (2 level tbsp) tomato paste
30 ml (2 level tbsp) flour
300 ml (½ pint) beef stock
2·5 ml (½ level tsp) dried rosemary
salt and freshly ground pepper

Trim excess fat from the cutlets. Heat the oil in a large frying pan and fry the cutlets for 10 minutes until golden brown on both sides. Remove from the pan and reserve. Add the onions, celery and mushrooms to the pan and fry for 6–10 minutes until golden brown. Add the tomatoes, tomato paste and flour and gradually add the stock. Bring to the boil and add the rosemary and seasoning. Pour the vegetables into the electric casserole and place the cutlets on top. Spoon some of the liquid over the cutlets to moisten them and place the lid in position. Cook on high for 3–4 hours or low for 6–8 hours.

Orange stuffed breast of lamb

Serve the lamb cut into thick slices with the orange sauce

2 large lean breasts of lamb, boned
4 medium-sized onions, skinned and sliced
10 ml (2 level tsp) flour
300 ml (½ pint) beef stock
5 ml (1 level tsp) demerara sugar
5 ml (1 tsp) Worcestershire sauce
grated rind and juice of 1 orange
salt and freshly ground pepper

For the stuffing
75 g (3 oz) fresh white breadcrumbs
grated rind of 1 orange
2·5 ml (½ level tsp) dried or freshly chopped mint
1 egg, beaten

Trim excess fat from the lamb. Stir the stuffing ingredients together and season well. Spread over the meat, roll up and tie with string. Cook the lamb in a frying pan without extra fat for 10 minutes until browned on all sides. Place the lamb in the electric casserole with the onion. Blend the flour to a smooth paste with a little stock and add to the electric casserole with the remaining ingredients. Place the lid in position and cook on high for 4–5 hours.

10 minutes before the end of cooking time cut the segments from the orange used in the stuffing. Add the orange segments to the electric casserole, replace the lid and continue cooking.

Hearty corn chowder (see page 19), Country lentil soup (see page 21)

Highland hot pot

30 ml (2 tbsp) vegetable oil
2 large carrots, peeled and chopped
1 large parsnip, peeled and chopped
2 sticks of celery, washed and chopped
1 medium-sized onion, skinned and chopped
45 ml (3 level tbsp) oatmeal
700 g (1 ½ lb) neck of lamb chops, trimmed
salt and freshly ground pepper
600 ml (1 pint) beef stock
15 g (½ oz) butter

Heat the oil in a frying pan, add the vegetables and cook for 5 minutes until soft. Transfer to the electric casserole. Using 30 ml (2 level tbsp) of seasoned oatmeal, coat each chop. Add to the pan and cook for 10 minutes until browned. Transfer to the electric casserole. Add the stock and seasoning to the pan, bring to the boil, stirring, and pour over the meat. Place the lid of the electric casserole in position and cook on high for 3–4 hours or low for 6–8 hours.

Just before serving melt the butter in a small pan, add the remaining oatmeal and cook for 5–8 minutes until golden brown. Sprinkle over the hot pot.

Steak and kidney pudding

Before you start, remember to check that your pudding basin fits into the earthenware casserole without touching the sides

For the filling
25 g (1 oz) lard
1 medium-sized onion, skinned and chopped
325 g (12 oz) braising steak, cubed
100 g (4 oz) lambs' or pigs' kidney, cored and
  diced
30 ml (2 level tbsp) flour
salt and freshly ground pepper

For the pastry
225 g (8 oz) self raising flour
2·5 ml (½ level tsp) salt
100 g (4 oz) shredded suet

To make the filling: melt the lard in a frying pan and fry the onion for 5 minutes until soft. Add the steak and kidney and fry for 10 minutes until browned. Sprinkle over the flour and plenty of seasoning and cook for 1–2 minutes, stirring.

Stir in 30 ml (2 tbsp) water and allow to cool slightly.

To make the pastry: sift the flour and salt together, add the suet and enough water to mix to a soft dough. Knead lightly on a floured board. Use two thirds of the pastry to line a greased 1·1-litre (2-pint) pudding basin. Add the filling and cover with the remaining pastry, sealing the edge well. Cover with greased greaseproof paper and foil and secure with string. Place in the electric casserole with boiling water to come halfway up the basin. Place the lid in position and cook on high for 4–6 hours.

✛ Savoury mince

Quick and easy to prepare – a useful standby for busy days

25 g (1 oz) butter or margarine
1 large onion, skinned and chopped
1 clove of garlic, skinned and crushed
900 g (2 lb) lean minced beef
30 ml (2 level tbsp) tomato paste
5 ml (1 level tsp) salt
freshly ground pepper

Melt the fat in a large frying pan and fry the onion and garlic for 5 minutes until beginning to brown. Add the mince and fry for 5 minutes until browned. Stir in the tomato paste and seasoning and transfer to the electric casserole. Place the lid in position and cook on high for 2–3 hours or low for 4–6 hours.

Cook double quantities – eat one and freeze one

✛ Southern beef and bean pot

100 g (4 oz) red kidney beans, soaked overnight
900 g (2 lb) lean chuck steak
salt and freshly ground pepper
25 g (1 oz) flour
45 ml (3 tbsp) vegetable oil
1 large onion, skinned and sliced
400 ml (¾ pint) beef stock
30 ml (2 level tbsp) tomato paste
1 bayleaf
thinly pared rind of ½ an orange

Soak the beans in cold water overnight and

Vegetable and bacon casserole (see page 33), Butter bean and vegetable stew (see page 37) drain. Trim the meat, cut into 2·5-cm (1-in) cubes and toss in seasoned flour. Heat the oil in a frying pan and cook the meat for 10 minutes until browned; transfer to the electric casserole. Add the onion to the frying pan and cook for 5 minutes until soft. Stir in the stock, tomato paste, beans, bayleaf, orange rind and seasoning. Bring to the boil, stirring, pour over the meat in the electric casserole and stir well. Place the lid in position and cook on high for 4–5 hours or low for 8–10 hours. Remove the orange rind before serving.

Beef and vegetable braise

An unusual combination of crunchy beef balls and tasty vegetables

30 ml (2 tbsp) vegetable oil
225 g (8 oz) carrots, peeled and diced
225 g (8 oz) leeks, thinly sliced and washed
225 g (8 oz) onions, skinned and sliced
225 g (8 oz) parsnips, peeled and diced
400 ml (¾ pint) beef stock
5 ml (1 level tsp) dried thyme
225 g (8 oz) lean minced beef
50 g (2 oz) fresh white breadcrumbs
25 g (1 oz) salted peanuts, finely chopped
25 g (1 oz) sultanas
15 ml (1 level tbsp) tomato paste
2·5 ml (½ level tsp) salt
freshly ground pepper
1 egg, beaten
15 ml (1 level tbsp) cornflour

Heat 15 ml (1 tbsp) oil in a large saucepan and fry the vegetables for 10 minutes until golden brown. Add the stock and thyme, bring to the boil and pour into the electric casserole. Mix together the minced beef, breadcrumbs, peanuts, sultanas, tomato paste, seasoning and beaten egg and shape into twelve balls.

Heat the remaining oil and fry the meat balls for 10 minutes until golden brown all over. Arrange them on top of the vegetables in the electric casserole and spoon a little liquid over the top. Place the lid in position and cook on high for 3–4 hours or low for 6–8 hours.

15 minutes before the end of cooking time blend the cornflour to a smooth paste with a

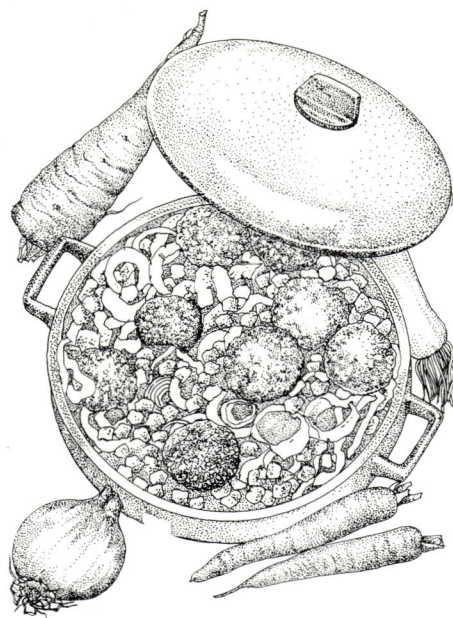

Beef and vegetable braise

little cold water and stir into the sauce. Replace the lid and continue cooking.

✦ Marinated brisket with vegetables

The spicy herb marinade enhances the natural flavour of the meat. The meat should be marinated overnight or for about 8 hours.

1·6-kg (3½-lb) piece boned and rolled brisket
8 peppercorns
6 cloves
2 bayleaves
2·5 ml (½ level tsp) dried rosemary
1 medium-sized onion, skinned and chopped
2 carrots, peeled and chopped
60 ml (4 tbsp) vegetable oil
60 ml (4 tbsp) vinegar
salt
25 g (1 oz) butter
300 ml (½ pint) beef stock
30 ml (2 level tbsp) cornflour

Wipe the meat and place in a large polythene bag or container. Crush the herbs and spices and add to the meat with the onion, carrots, oil, vinegar and salt. Marinate overnight.

Melt the butter in a frying pan, add the drained meat and cook for 10 minutes until browned all over. Transfer to the electric casserole, pour the marinade and stock into the pan, bring to the boil and pour over the meat in the electric casserole. Place the lid in position and cook on high for 5–6 hours or low for 10–12 hours.

Remove the meat from the electric casserole and place on a hot serving dish. Drain any excess fat from the juices. Blend the cornflour to a smooth paste with a little meat juice, add to the electric casserole. Cut the meat into thick slices. Strain the gravy and serve with the meat.

✤ Beef goulash

Buttered noodles and broccoli make a good accompaniment to this spiced beef recipe

450 g (1 lb) stewing steak
salt and freshly ground pepper
45 ml (3 level tbsp) flour
25 g (1 oz) butter or margarine
2 medium-sized onions, skinned and chopped
1 red pepper, seeded and chopped
10 ml (2 level tsp) paprika
100 g (4 oz) button mushrooms, halved
60 ml (4 level tbsp) tomato paste
1·25 ml (¼ level tsp) caraway seeds
a little grated nutmeg
600 ml (1 pint) beef stock
bouquet garni
142-ml (5-fl oz) carton soured cream

Cut the meat into 2·5-cm (1-in) cubes and coat in seasoned flour. Melt the fat in a pan, add the onions and pepper and cook for 5 minutes. Add the meat and cook for 5–10 minutes until well browned. Add the paprika and mushrooms and cook for a further 1 minute. Stir in the tomato paste, seasonings and any remaining flour. Gradually stir in the stock, add the bouquet garni and bring to the boil. Pour into the electric casserole and stir well. Place the lid in position and cook on high for 4–5 hours or low for 8–10 hours.

Just before serving remove the bouquet garni and stir in the soured cream.
Freeze without the soured cream

✤ Beef curry

A traditional fruity curry to serve with turmeric rice and mango chutney

30 ml (2 tbsp) vegetable oil
700 g (1½ lb) stewing steak, cubed
2 large onions, skinned and sliced
1 cooking apple, peeled, cored and chopped
15 ml (1 level tbsp) curry powder
45 ml (3 level tbsp) flour
600 ml (1 pint) beef stock
salt and freshly ground pepper
30 ml (2 level tbsp) chutney
50 g (2 oz) sultanas
2 tomatoes, skinned and chopped
5 ml (1 tsp) lemon juice

Heat the oil in a frying pan and fry the meat for 10 minutes until browned. Drain and place in the electric casserole. Add the onions and apple to the pan and cook for 5 minutes. Stir in the curry powder and flour and cook for 1 minute. Gradually stir in the stock, seasoning and remaining ingredients. Bring to the boil and pour into the electric casserole. Stir well and place the lid in position. Cook on high for 4–5 hours or low for 8–10 hours.

✤ Beef and lentil stew

100 g (4 oz) red lentils, soaked overnight
30 ml (2 tbsp) vegetable oil
450 g (1 lb) braising steak, cut into 2·5-cm (1-in) cubes
1 large onion, skinned and sliced
2 carrots, peeled and diced
400 ml (¾ pint) beef stock
5 ml (1 level tsp) salt
freshly ground pepper
2·5 ml (½ level tsp) dry mustard
5 ml (1 tsp) Worcestershire sauce
396-g (14-oz) can tomatoes
2·5 ml (½ level tsp) dried mixed herbs
1 bayleaf
2·5 ml (½ level tsp) sugar

Soak the lentils overnight and drain. Heat the oil in a frying pan and cook the meat for 10 minutes until browned. Place in the electric casserole. Add the onion and carrots to the pan and cook for 5 minutes until soft. Stir in the lentils, stock and remaining ingredients and bring to the boil. Pour into the electric casserole and stir well. Place the lid in position and cook on high for 4–5 hours or low for 8–10 hours.

✤ Beef casserole with cauliflower

You will find that the cauliflower keeps its nice crunchy texture in this casserole dish

700 g (1 ½ lb) stewing steak
15 ml (1 tbsp) vegetable oil
1 onion, skinned and chopped
1 clove of garlic, skinned and crushed
2 carrots, peeled and sliced
30 ml (2 level tbsp) flour
600 ml (1 pint) beef stock
10 ml (2 tsp) soy sauce
5 ml (1 level tsp) dried mixed herbs
salt and freshly ground pepper
225 g (8 oz) tomatoes, skinned and quartered
100 g (4 oz) button mushrooms
1 large cauliflower, cut into florets

Cut the meat into 2·5-cm (1-in) cubes. Heat the oil in a frying pan and fry the meat, onion and garlic for 10 minutes until golden brown. Add the carrots and cook for a further 2 minutes. Transfer to the electric casserole. Stir the flour into the remaining oil in the pan and gradually add the stock. Bring to the boil and add the soy sauce, mixed herbs, seasoning and vegetables. Place in the electric casserole and place the lid in position. Cook on high for 4–5 hours or low for 8–10 hours.

Chicken with courgettes and pineapple

The courgettes, pineapple and orange juice add a refreshing flavour to this casserole

30 ml (2 tbsp) vegetable oil
4 chicken portions, skinned
1 medium-sized onion, skinned and chopped
450 g (1 lb) courgettes, trimmed and sliced
198-g (7-oz) can pineapple slices
150 ml (¼ pint) chicken stock
15 ml (1 tbsp) soy sauce
15 ml (1 level tbsp) tomato paste
salt and freshly ground pepper
15 ml (1 level tbsp) cornflour
juice of 1 small orange

Chicken with courgettes and pineapple

Heat the oil in a frying pan and cook the chicken for 10 minutes until golden brown. Remove from the pan and place in the electric casserole. Add the onion and courgettes to the pan and cook for 5 minutes until soft. Mix the pineapple syrup, stock, soy sauce, tomato paste, seasoning and cornflour with the orange juice to make a smooth paste. Add to the pan and bring to the boil, stirring. Place a pineapple slice on each chicken portion. Pour the sauce over the chicken, place the lid in position and cook on high for 3–4 hours or low for 6–8 hours.

Mexican chicken

225 g (8 oz) aubergines
25 g (1 oz) butter or margarine
4 chicken portions, skinned
2 medium-sized onions, skinned and chopped
225-g (8-oz) can tomatoes
15 ml (1 tbsp) vinegar
10 ml (2 level tsp) demerara sugar
10 ml (2 level tsp) dry mustard
30 ml (2 tbsp) Worcestershire sauce
pinch of chilli powder
freshly ground pepper

Trim and slice the aubergines. Melt the fat in a frying pan and cook the chicken for 10 minutes until browned. Place in the electric casserole. Add the aubergines and onions to the pan and cook for 5 minutes until soft. Add the remaining ingredients, bring to the boil and pour over the chicken in the electric casserole. Place the lid in position and cook on high for 3–4 hours or low for 6–8 hours.

✢ Chicken and bean hot pot

225 g (8 oz) butter beans, soaked overnight
30 ml (2 tbsp) vegetable oil
4 chicken portions, skinned
1 large onion, skinned and chopped
2 sticks of celery, washed and chopped
2 carrots, peeled and chopped
30 ml (2 level tbsp) flour
600 ml (1 pint) chicken stock
15 ml (1 level tbsp) peanut butter
2·5 ml (½ level tsp) English mustard
salt and freshly ground pepper
15 ml (1 tbsp) freshly chopped chives

Soak the beans overnight and drain. Heat the oil in a frying pan and fry the chicken for 10 minutes until golden brown. Remove from the pan and place in the electric casserole. Add the onion, celery and carrots to the pan and cook for 10 minutes until golden brown. Add the beans, cook for a further minute and place in the electric casserole. Stir the flour into the remaining fat in the pan. Add the stock and the remaining ingredients. Bring to the boil, pour into the electric casserole and stir well. Place the lid in position and cook on high for 3–4 hours or low for 6–8 hours.

✢ Summer braised chicken

Use fresh young vegetables for this summer casserole. If only larger vegetables are available cut them into small pieces before adding to the electric casserole

4 chicken portions, skinned
salt and freshly ground pepper
45 ml (3 level tbsp) flour
25 g (1 oz) butter
15 ml (1 tbsp) vegetable oil
450 g (1 lb) small new potatoes, scraped
325 g (12 oz) small new carrots, scraped
2 medium-sized onions, skinned and chopped
300 ml (½ pint) chicken stock
a few sprigs of fresh thyme or 5 ml (1 level tsp) dried thyme
grated rind and juice of 1 lemon
freshly chopped thyme to garnish

Coat the chicken in seasoned flour. Heat the butter and oil in a frying pan and cook the chicken for 10 minutes until golden brown. Transfer to the electric casserole. Add the vegetables to the frying pan and cook for 5–8 minutes, until beginning to colour. Stir in the stock, thyme, lemon rind and juice and seasoning. Bring to the boil, stirring, and pour over the chicken. Place the lid in position and cook on high for 3–4 hours or low for 6–8 hours. Remove the thyme sprigs. Serve garnished with freshly chopped thyme.

NOTE Chicken is best skinned before cooking in an electric casserole to minimise the amount of fat in the finished dish.

✤ Chicken and mushroom casserole

If shallots are unobtainable use small pickling onions or onion slices instead

30 ml (2 tbsp) vegetable oil
4 chicken portions, skinned
100 g (4 oz) streaky bacon, rinded and chopped
225 g (8 oz) shallots, skinned
225 g (8 oz) button mushrooms
45 ml (3 level tbsp) flour
300 ml (½ pint) chicken stock
150 ml (¼ pint) dry cider
salt and freshly ground pepper
5 ml (1 level tsp) French mustard
5 ml (1 tsp) Worcestershire sauce
2·5 ml (½ level tsp) dried basil

Heat the oil in a frying pan and fry the chicken joints for 10 minutes until golden brown. Remove from the pan and place in the electric casserole. Add the bacon and shallots to the pan and cook for 10 minutes until golden brown. Add the mushrooms, fry for a further 2 minutes and place in the electric casserole. Stir the flour into the remaining fat in the pan and gradually stir in the stock and cider. Add the remaining ingredients and bring to the boil. Pour over the chicken and vegetables in the electric casserole. Place the lid in position and cook on high for 3–4 hours or low for 6–8 hours.

✤ Poacher's pot

Rabbit casseroled in a mustard flavoured sauce

700 g (1½ lb) rabbit
15 ml (1 level tbsp) flour
25 g (1 oz) butter
1 small onion, skinned and chopped
30 ml (2 level tbsp) demerara sugar
5 ml (1 level tsp) tomato paste
10 ml (2 level tsp) dry mustard
400 ml (¾ pint) chicken stock
60 ml (4 tbsp) malt vinegar
5 ml (1 tsp) soy sauce
15 ml (1 tbsp) lemon juice
salt and freshly ground pepper

Wipe the rabbit, cut into twelve pieces and toss in the flour. Melt the butter in a large frying pan and fry the rabbit for 10 minutes until browned.

Remove from the pan and place in the electric casserole. Add the onion to the pan and fry for 5 minutes, until soft. Stir in the sugar, tomato paste, mustard and stock. Bring to the boil and add the remaining ingredients. Pour into the casserole, place the lid in position and cook on high for 3–4 hours or low for 6–8 hours.

Spring casserole

4 spare rib pork chops
15 ml (1 tbsp) vegetable oil
1 medium-sized onion, skinned and sliced
450 g (1 lb) new carrots, scraped
450 g (1 lb) small new potatoes, scraped
30 ml (2 level tbsp) flour
300 ml (½ pint) chicken stock
2·5 ml (½ level tsp) dried mixed herbs
salt and freshly ground black pepper
freshly chopped parsley

Trim excess fat from the chops. Heat the oil in a frying pan and fry the chops for 10 minutes until brown on both sides. Transfer them to the electric casserole. Add the onion, carrots and potatoes to the frying pan and cook for 5 minutes. Stir in the flour and cook for 1 minute. Gradually stir in the stock, herbs and seasoning, bring to the boil and pour into the electric casserole. Place the lid in position and cook on high for 3–4 hours or low for 6–8 hours. Serve garnished with parsley.

Pork chops with red cabbage

The red cabbage absorbs the flavour of the pork and cider

700 g (1½ lb) red cabbage
50 g (2 oz) butter
1 large onion, skinned and finely chopped
1 clove of garlic, skinned and crushed
salt and freshly ground pepper
5 ml (1 level tsp) ground nutmeg
4 spare rib pork chops
30 ml (2 level tbsp) cornflour
300 ml (½ pint) dry cider
150 ml (¼ pint) chicken stock
ground nutmeg

Shred the cabbage finely and blanch it in boiling salted water for 2–3 minutes. Drain and turn into a bowl. Melt half the butter in a frying pan and cook the onion and garlic for 5 minutes until soft. Add the onion mixture to the cabbage with seasoning and nutmeg and toss well. Place in the electric casserole. Heat the remaining butter in the pan and fry the chops for 5–10 minutes until golden brown. Put them on top of the cabbage in the electric casserole and season. Blend the cornflour to a smooth paste with the cider, add to the pan with the stock and bring to the boil, stirring. Pour over the chops in the electric casserole and sprinkle with nutmeg. Place the lid in position and cook on high for 3–4 hours or low for 6–8 hours.

Spiced spare rib chops

Most butchers sell spare rib pork chops. The meat is sweet and succulent and often overlooked in favour of more expensive chops

30 ml (2 tbsp) vegetable oil
4 spare rib pork chops
1 large onion, skinned and sliced
15 ml (1 level tbsp) cornflour
30 ml (2 level tbsp) tomato paste
5 ml (1 level tsp) dry mustard
5 ml (1 level tsp) ground ginger
15 ml (1 tbsp) Worcestershire sauce
15 ml (1 tbsp) vinegar
15 ml (1 level tbsp) brown sugar
15 ml (1 tbsp) lemon juice
salt and freshly ground pepper
300 ml (½ pint) chicken stock

Pork chops with red cabbage

Heat the oil in a frying pan and cook the chops for 10 minutes until browned on both sides. Remove from the pan and place in the electric casserole. Add the onion and cook for 5 minutes until soft. Blend the cornflour to a smooth paste with the tomato paste and remaining ingredients except the stock, then gradually blend in the stock. Add to the pan and bring to the boil, stirring. Pour over the chops in the casserole. Place the lid in position and cook on high for 3–4 hours or low for 6–8 hours.

Lemon stuffed pork chops with walnuts

4 thick boneless pork chops
30 ml (2 tbsp) vegetable oil
2 cooking apples, peeled, cored and sliced
1 large onion, skinned and sliced
2 sticks of celery, washed and chopped
50 g (2 oz) walnuts, chopped
15 ml (1 level tbsp) flour
150 ml (¼ pint) chicken stock
salt and freshly ground pepper
142-ml (5-fl oz) carton soured cream

For the stuffing
100 g (4 oz) fresh white breadcrumbs
15 ml (1 tbsp) freshly chopped parsley
10 ml (2 tsp) freshly chopped chives
grated rind and juice of 1 lemon
salt and freshly ground pepper

Cut each chop horizontally without cutting right through to make a pocket for the stuffing. Stir the stuffing ingredients together and divide between the four chops. Secure each stuffed chop with a wooden cocktail stick. Heat the oil in a frying pan and fry the chops for 5 minutes on each side until golden brown. Remove from the pan and reserve. Add the apples, onion and celery and fry them for 3–4 minutes, add the walnuts and flour and then gradually stir in the stock. Bring to the boil and season. Pour the vegetables into the electric casserole and place the chops on top. Spoon some of the liquid over the chops, place the lid in position and cook on high for 3–4 hours or low for 6–8 hours.

15 minutes before the end of cooking time stir in the soured cream. Remove the cocktail sticks before serving.

Spiced pork with parsley dumplings

450 g (1 lb) lean belly of pork
45 ml (3 tbsp) vegetable oil
1 large onion, skinned and sliced
4 medium-sized carrots, peeled and quartered
2 sticks of celery, washed and chopped
15 ml (1 level tbsp) flour
5 ml (1 level tsp) ground coriander
2.5 ml (½ level tsp) ground cummin
salt and freshly ground pepper
700 ml (1¼ pints) chicken stock

For the dumplings
100 g (4 oz) self raising flour
50 g (2 oz) shredded suet
30 ml (2 tbsp) freshly chopped parsley

Cut the pork into strips discarding the skin and bone. Heat the oil in a frying pan and fry the meat for 10 minutes until golden brown. Add the vegetables and cook for a further 5 minutes. Stir in the flour, spices and seasoning and cook for 1 minute. Gradually stir in the stock and bring to the boil. Pour into the electric casserole and place the lid in position. Cook on high for 3–4 hours or low for 6–8 hours.

45 minutes before the end of cooking time turn the electric casserole to high. Stir the dumpling ingredients together with enough cold water to bind. Shape into eight even-sized balls and add them to the casserole. Replace the lid and continue cooking.

Pork and pineapple casserole

Serve with a green salad or buttered French beans

30 ml (2 tbsp) vegetable oil
700 g (1½ lb) spare rib pork chops
2 medium-sized onions, skinned and chopped
1 medium-sized green pepper, seeded and chopped
100 g (4 oz) button mushrooms
30 ml (2 level tbsp) flour
150 ml (¼ pint) chicken stock
150 ml (¼ pint) dry cider
210-g (7½-oz) can pineapple pieces
15 ml (1 tbsp) redcurrant jelly
salt and freshly ground pepper

Heat the oil in a frying pan and fry the chops for 10 minutes until golden brown. Remove from the pan, drain on kitchen paper towel and reserve. Add the onions, pepper and mushrooms to the pan and fry them for 5 minutes until golden brown. Add the flour then gradually stir in the stock, cider and pineapple juice. Bring to the boil then add the pineapple pieces, redcurrant jelly and seasoning. Pour the vegetables into the electric casserole and place the chops on top. Spoon some of the liquid over the chops and place the lid in position. Cook on high for 3–4 hours or low for 6–8 hours.

Apple and walnut stuffed pork roll

1·1 kg (2 ½ lb) belly of pork, boned
15 ml (1 tbsp) vegetable oil
225 g (8 oz) carrots, peeled and sliced
225 g (8 oz) onion, skinned and chopped
600 ml (1 pint) chicken stock
15 ml (1 tbsp) Worcestershire sauce
salt and freshly ground pepper
30 ml (2 level tbsp) cornflour

For the stuffing
100 g (4 oz) fresh white breadcrumbs
1 large apple, peeled, cored and grated
grated rind of 1 lemon
7·5 ml (1 ½ level tsp) dried sage
1 small onion, skinned and finely chopped
salt and freshly ground pepper
25 g (1 oz) walnuts, chopped
1 large egg, beaten

Mix all the ingredients for the stuffing together and bind with the beaten egg. Place the pork skin side down and spread evenly with the stuffing. Roll up and tie securely with string. Score the skin with a sharp knife. Heat the oil in a frying pan and fry the meat for 10 minutes until well browned on all sides. Remove the meat from the pan and reserve. Add the vegetables to the pan and fry them for 10 minutes until they are browned. Stir in the stock, Worcestershire sauce and seasoning and bring to the boil. Mix the cornflour to a smooth paste with a little water and add to the pan. Bring back to the boil and cook for 1 minute. Pour the

vegetables into the electric casserole and place the meat on top. Place the lid in position and cook on high for 4–5 hours.

To serve: remove the string and slice off the skin. Cook the skin under a hot grill for 2–3 minutes until it is golden brown and crisp. Slice the meat into eight to ten slices and serve with the vegetables and the gravy.

✚ Braised lambs' liver

Use red wine for special occasions, beef stock for everyday

45 ml (3 tbsp) vegetable oil
450 g (1 lb) lambs' liver, sliced
100 g (4 oz) streaky bacon, rinded and chopped
1 large onion, skinned and sliced
1 clove of garlic, skinned and crushed
15 ml (1 level tbsp) cornflour
150 ml (¼ pint) beef stock
150 ml (¼ pint) red wine or beef stock
30 ml (2 tbsp) freshly chopped parsley
2·5 ml (½ level tsp) salt

Heat the oil in a frying pan and fry the liver for 5 minutes until brown. Drain and reserve. Fry the bacon, onion and garlic for 5 minutes, until the onion is soft. Blend the cornflour with the stock and wine and add to the pan, stirring. Add the parsley and seasoning. Bring to the boil, stirring. Pour into the electric casserole with the liver. Place the lid in position and cook on high for 2–3 hours or low for 4–6 hours.

Ox heart ragoût

A rich and tasty way of cooking ox heart – and economical too

900 g (2 lb) ox heart
50 g (2 oz) butter or margarine
1 large onion, skinned and chopped
50 g (2 oz) streaky bacon, rinded and chopped
45 ml (3 level tbsp) flour
15 ml (1 level tbsp) paprika
300 ml (½ pint) beef stock
150 ml (¼ pint) red wine or beef stock
salt and freshly ground pepper
75 g (3 oz) pasta shapes

Trim the tubes and fat from the meat and wash

well. Cut into 2·5-cm (1-in) pieces. Melt the fat in a frying pan and fry the meat, onion and bacon together for 5–7 minutes until they begin to brown. Stir in the flour and paprika and fry for 1–2 minutes. Gradually stir in the stock, wine and seasoning and bring to the boil. Transfer everything to the electric casserole. Place the lid in position and cook on high for 3–4 hours or low for 6–8 hours.

45 minutes before the end of cooking time turn the electric casserole to high. Stir in the pasta shapes, replace the lid and continue cooking.

Oxtail and vegetable braise

A wholesome economical casserole using a variety of winter vegetables

1 whole oxtail, jointed and trimmed
25 g (1 oz) flour
15 ml (1 tbsp) vegetable oil
25 g (1 oz) butter
1 large onion, skinned and chopped
2–3 medium-sized carrots, peeled and chopped
100 g (4 oz) swede, peeled and chopped
1 small turnip, peeled and chopped
2 sticks of celery, washed and chopped
1 large potato, peeled and chopped
1 clove of garlic, skinned and crushed
600 ml (1 pint) beef stock
30 ml (2 level tbsp) tomato paste
1·25 ml (¼ level tsp) dried mixed herbs
salt and freshly ground pepper
100 g (4 oz) button mushrooms
15 ml (1 level tbsp) cornflour
freshly chopped parsley to garnish

Toss the oxtail in seasoned flour. Heat the oil and butter in a frying pan, add the oxtail and fry for 10 minutes until brown. Transfer to the electric casserole. Add the vegetables and garlic to the frying pan and fry for 5 minutes, until soft, then gradually stir in the stock, tomato paste, herbs and seasoning. Bring to the boil, stirring. Pour over the oxtail in the electric casserole, add the mushrooms and stir well. Place the lid in position and cook on high for 4–5 hours or low for 8–10 hours.

Just before serving blend the cornflour to a smooth paste with a little cold water and stir into the electric casserole. Replace the lid and continue cooking for a few minutes. Serve garnished with parsley.

Rich tripe casserole

An economical family meal

700 g (1½ lb) tripe
25 g (1 oz) butter or margarine
1 small onion, skinned and chopped
1 carrot, peeled and chopped
50 g (2 oz) bacon, rinded and chopped
30 ml (2 level tbsp) flour
15 ml (1 level tbsp) tomato paste
400 ml (¾ pint) beef stock
5 ml (1 tsp) lemon juice
50 g (2 oz) mushrooms, sliced
salt and freshly ground pepper
freshly chopped parsley

Place the tripe in a large saucepan and cover with cold water. Bring to the boil, drain, rinse in cold water and then cut tripe into strips about 3·5 by 1 cm (1½ by ½ in). Melt the fat in a frying pan and fry the onion, carrot and bacon for 5 minutes, until soft. Stir in the flour and cook for 1–2 minutes, until brown. Stir in the tomato paste, stock, lemon juice, mushrooms and seasoning. Bring to the boil and transfer to the electric casserole together with the tripe. Place the lid in position and cook on high for 3–4 hours or low for 6–8 hours. Serve garnished with parsley.

✤ Liver and vegetable hot pot

25 g (1 oz) butter
450 g (1 lb) potatoes, peeled and thinly sliced
100 g (4 oz) carrots, peeled and sliced
1 large onion, skinned and sliced
100 g (4 oz) mushrooms
2 sticks of celery, washed and chopped
450 g (1 lb) lamb's liver
salt and freshly ground pepper
25 g (1 oz) flour
100 g (4 oz) streaky bacon, rinded and chopped
300 ml (½ pint) beef stock
5 ml (1 tsp) Worcestershire sauce
15 ml (1 level tbsp) tomato paste

Melt the butter in a frying pan, add the vegetables and fry for 5–8 minutes. Drain them on paper towel and transfer to the electric casserole. Cut the liver into 2·5-cm (1-in) strips and coat in seasoned flour. Add to the pan with the bacon and fry for 5 minutes. Gradually stir in the stock with the Worcestershire sauce, seasoning and tomato paste. Bring to the boil, stirring, transfer to the electric casserole and stir well. Place the lid in position and cook on high for 2–3 hours or low for 4–6 hours.

Catalan style haddock

Spicy and tasty with capers and black olives

four 175-g (6-oz) haddock steaks
25 g (1 oz) butter
15 ml (1 tbsp) vegetable oil
1 large onion, skinned and sliced
60 ml (4 level tbsp) tomato paste
30 ml (2 level tbsp) flour
300 ml (½ pint) fish or chicken stock
150 ml (¼ pint) dry white wine
25 g (1 oz) anchovies, drained and chopped
50 g (2 oz) black olives
25 g (1 oz) capers
salt and freshly ground black pepper

Wipe the fish, remove the fins and black skin

and place in the electric casserole. Heat the butter and oil in a frying pan. Add the onion and fry for 5 minutes, until soft. Add the tomato paste and flour and cook for 1 minute, stirring. Gradually stir in the stock, wine, anchovies, olives, capers and seasoning. Bring to the boil, stirring, and pour the sauce over the fish in the electric casserole. Place the lid in position and cook on high for 1½–2 hours or on low for 3–4 hours.

Haddock hot pot

A complete fish dish. Follow the cooking times carefully to avoid overcooking the fish

15 ml (1 tbsp) vegetable oil
1 large onion, skinned and chopped
2 sticks of celery, washed and chopped
225 g (8 oz) potatoes, peeled and thinly sliced
225 g (8 oz) tomatoes, skinned and quartered
225 g (8 oz) button mushrooms
300 ml (½ pint) fish or chicken stock
450 g (1 lb) fresh haddock, skinned and cubed
salt and cayenne pepper
freshly chopped parsley

Heat the oil in a large saucepan and fry the

Catalan style haddock

onion, celery and potatoes for 5 minutes until softened. Add the tomatoes and mushrooms and cook for a further 2–3 minutes. Stir in the stock, add the fish, season and bring to the boil. Pour everything into the electric casserole. Place the lid in position and cook on high for 2½–3 hours or low for 5–6 hours. Serve sprinkled with parsley.

Coley with oriental sauce

Coley is relatively economical. For grander occasions use cod or haddock

25 g (1 oz) butter
1 large onion, skinned and chopped
1 clove of garlic, skinned and crushed
3 sticks of celery, washed and thinly sliced
63-g (2¼-oz) can tomato paste
45 ml (3 level tbsp) concentrated curry sauce
400 ml (¾ pint) fish or chicken stock
50 g (2 oz) sultanas
25 g (1 oz) desiccated coconut
1 large piece of stem ginger, finely chopped
30 ml (2 level tbsp) redcurrant jelly
15 ml (1 level tbsp) cornflour
30 ml (2 tbsp) lemon juice
900 g (2 lb) coley fillet, skinned

Melt the butter in a frying pan, add the onions, garlic and celery and cook for 5 minutes, until soft. Stir in the tomato paste, curry sauce, stock, sultanas, coconut, ginger and redcurrant jelly. Bring to the boil, stirring. Blend the cornflour to a smooth paste with the lemon juice and a little water and stir into the sauce. Bring back to the boil and cook for 1 minute. Wipe the fish, remove any bones and cut into large chunks. Place in the electric casserole, pour the sauce over the fish and stir well. Place the lid in position and cook on high for 1½–2 hours or low for 3–4 hours.

Cod à la provençale

15 ml (1 tbsp) vegetable oil
225 g (8 oz) shallots, skinned
1 clove of garlic, skinned and crushed
450 g (1 lb) tomatoes, skinned and chopped
15 ml (1 level tbsp) tomato paste
60 ml (4 tbsp) white wine or stock
salt and freshly ground pepper
2·5 ml (½ level tsp) dried thyme
15 ml (1 tbsp) freshly chopped parsley
700 g (1½ lb) cod fillet, skinned and cubed

Heat the oil in a saucepan and fry the shallots and garlic for 10 minutes until lightly browned. Add the remaining ingredients and bring to the boil, stirring. Pour into the electric casserole and place the lid in position. Cook on high for 2–3 hours or low for 4–6 hours.

Easy entertaining

✤ Summer braised loin of lamb

1 loin of lamb, boned
15 ml (1 tbsp) vegetable oil
1 large onion, skinned and chopped
225 g (8 oz) small carrots, peeled
3 sticks of celery, washed and sliced
225 g (8 oz) courgettes, trimmed and sliced
225 g (8 oz) tomatoes, skinned and quartered
30 ml (2 level tbsp) flour
400 ml (¾ pint) beef stock
2·5 ml (½ tsp) freshly chopped thyme
salt and freshly ground pepper

Trim excess fat from the lamb, roll up neatly and tie with string. Heat the oil in a frying pan and fry the lamb for 10 minutes until browned. Remove from the pan and reserve. Add the onion, carrots and celery to the pan and cook for 5 minutes. Add the courgettes and tomatoes and cook for 1 minute. Stir in the flour, add the stock, thyme and seasoning and bring to the boil. Pour into the electric casserole and place the lamb on top. Spoon a little stock over the lamb. Place the lid in position and cook on high for 4–5 hours or low for 8–10 hours. Remove the string before serving.

✤ Marinated lamb with oranges

1 lean shoulder of lamb, boned and trimmed
300 ml (½ pint) red wine
1 medium-sized onion, skinned and chopped
1 carrot, peeled and chopped
1 stick of celery, washed and chopped
2 rashers of streaky bacon, rinded and chopped
2 cloves of garlic, skinned and crushed
1 bayleaf
2·5 ml (½ level tsp) dried thyme
2 large oranges
15 ml (1 tbsp) vegetable oil
25 g (1 oz) butter
30 ml (2 level tbsp) flour
600 ml (1 pint) beef stock
30 ml (2 level tbsp) tomato paste
50 g (2 oz) button mushrooms
salt and freshly ground pepper
freshly chopped parsley to garnish

Cut the lamb into 2·5-cm (1-in) cubes and place in a bowl with the wine, prepared vegetables, bacon, garlic and herbs. Remove the rind from the oranges and add to the marinade. Cover and leave in a cool place for 30 minutes.

Cut the oranges into segments and reserve. Drain the marinade from the meat and vegetables and reserve. Heat the oil and butter in a frying pan and fry the meat and vegetables for 10 minutes until golden brown. Place in the electric casserole. Add the flour to the pan and cook for 2 minutes, stirring. Gradually stir in the stock and tomato paste and bring to the boil. Add the marinade, mushrooms and seasoning, pour over the meat in the electric casserole and stir well. Place the lid in position and cook on high for 3–4 hours or low for 6–8 hours.

Just before serving, remove the orange rind, stir in the orange segments and sprinkle with parsley.

✤ Fruity lamb casserole

Deliciously different − casseroled lamb with plump apricots and prunes. Serve with boiled rice or sauté potatoes

700 g (1½ lb) shoulder of lamb, boned
2·5 ml (½ level tsp) salt
freshly ground black pepper
30 ml (2 level tbsp) flour
15 ml (1 tbsp) vegetable oil
50 g (2 oz) prunes, stoned and halved
50 g (2 oz) dried apricots
150 ml (¼ pint) beef stock
15 ml (1 tbsp) vinegar
25 g (1 oz) brown sugar
1·25 ml (¼ level tsp) ground cinnamon

Trim the lamb, remove the excess fat and cut into 2·5-cm (1-in) cubes. Toss in seasoned flour. Heat the oil in a frying pan and fry the meat for 10 minutes until browned. Stir in any flour left over and cook for 1 minute. Stir in the remaining ingredients, bring to the boil and transfer to the electric casserole. Place the lid in position and cook on high for 3–4 hours or low for 6–8 hours.

✤ Lamb and mushrooms in red wine

1·1 kg (2 ½ lb) lean leg of lamb, boned
45 ml (3 tbsp) vegetable oil
2 medium-sized onions, skinned and chopped
1 clove of garlic, skinned and crushed
225 g (8 oz) button mushrooms
300 ml (½ pint) red wine
150 ml (¼ pint) beef stock
salt and freshly ground pepper
15 ml (1 level tbsp) cornflour
freshly chopped parsley and croûtons to garnish

Trim the lamb and cut into 2·5-cm (1-in) pieces. Heat the oil in a frying pan and fry the lamb for 10 minutes until brown. Place in the electric casserole. Add the onions and garlic to the pan and cook for 5 minutes. Add the mushrooms and cook for 1 minute. Add the remaining ingredients except the cornflour and bring to the boil. Pour into the electric casserole and stir well. Place the lid in position and cook on high for 3–4 hours or low for 6–8 hours.

5 minutes before the end of cooking time blend the cornflour to a smooth paste with a little cold water, stir into the casserole, replace the lid and continue cooking. Serve garnished with parsley and croûtons.

Shoulder of lamb à la provençale

Lamb rolled and stuffed with garlic and anchovies and cooked in a red wine sauce with tomatoes

1·5 kg (3 lb) shoulder of lamb, boned
salt and freshly ground pepper
30 ml (2 tbsp) vegetable oil
2 large onions, skinned and thinly sliced
225 g (8 oz) tomatoes, skinned and sliced
150 ml (¼ pint) beef stock
150 ml (¼ pint) red wine

For the stuffing
15 ml (1 tbsp) vegetable oil
½ small onion, skinned and chopped
1 clove of garlic, skinned and crushed
2 anchovy fillets, crushed
75 g (3 oz) fresh white breadcrumbs
1 egg, beaten

Trim excess fat from the lamb and season well.

To make the stuffing: heat the oil in a pan add the onion and garlic and fry for 5 minutes. Stir in the remaining ingredients, season and add enough egg to bind. Spread the stuffing over the lamb, roll up and tie neatly with string. Heat the oil in a frying pan and fry the lamb roll for 10 minutes, until browned all over. Reserve. Add the onions and tomatoes to the pan and cook for 5 minutes. Add the stock, wine and seasoning and bring to the boil. Pour into the electric casserole. Place the lamb roll on top and spoon some of the juice over it. Place the lid in position and cook on high for 4–5 hours or low for 8–10 hours.

At the end of the cooking time remove the lamb, cut away the string and serve with the vegetables.
SERVES 6

✤ Lamb fillet with lemon and garlic

Escalopes made from lamb fillet, cooked in a tangy lemon and basil sauce

700 g (1 ½ lb) lamb fillet
salt and freshly ground pepper
30 ml (2 level tbsp) flour
30 ml (2 tbsp) vegetable oil
1 large onion, skinned and chopped
1 clove of garlic, skinned and crushed
grated rind and juice of 1 lemon
300 ml (½ pint) beef stock
2·5 ml (½ level tsp) dried basil
141-g (5-oz) carton natural yogurt
freshly chopped basil (optional)
lemon slices to garnish

Cut the fillets in half crosswise then split in half lengthways. Beat out with a rolling pin to make escalopes of even thickness. Toss in seasoned flour. Heat the oil in a frying pan and fry the meat for 10 minutes until browned on both sides. Reserve. Add the onion and garlic to the pan and fry for 5 minutes. Add the lemon rind and juice, stock, basil and seasoning and bring to the boil. Pour into the electric casserole, place the escalopes on top and spoon some sauce over them. Place the lid in position and cook on high for 2–3 hours or low for 4–6 hours.

Just before serving stir in the yogurt and freshly chopped basil and serve garnished with lemon slices.

Freeze without the yogurt and herbs

✤ Lamb noisettes in sherry sauce

ILLUSTRATED IN COLOUR ON THE JACKET

It is helpful to give your butcher advance warning so he has time to prepare the noisettes

8 noisettes of lamb
salt and freshly ground pepper
30 ml (2 tbsp) vegetable oil
100 g (4 oz) carrots, peeled and diced
1 medium-sized onion, skinned and chopped
2 sticks of celery, washed and chopped
300 ml (½ pint) beef stock
15 ml (1 level tbsp) tomato paste
30 ml (2 level tbsp) redcurrant jelly
30 ml (2 tbsp) sherry
watercress sprigs to garnish

Season the noisettes on both sides. Heat the oil in. a frying pan and fry the noisettes for 10 minutes until browned on both sides. Remove from the pan and reserve. Add the vegetables to the pan and cook for 5 minutes. Stir in the remaining ingredients and bring to the boil. Pour into the electric casserole, place the noisettes on top and spoon over a little stock. Place the lid in position and cook on high for 3–4 hours or low for 6–8 hours.

Serve the noisettes on a heated dish garnished with watercress. Rub the sauce through a sieve or purée in a blender. Spoon some of the sauce over the noisettes and serve the remainder separately.

Freeze with the sauce

✤ Spanish lamb casserole

Serve this colourful lamb casserole with rice or creamed potatoes

700 g (1½ lb) lean shoulder of lamb, boned
salt and freshly ground pepper
45 ml (3 level tbsp) flour
30 ml (2 tbsp) vegetable oil
1 clove of garlic, skinned and crushed
1 green pepper, seeded and chopped
4 sticks of celery, washed and chopped
300 ml (½ pint) beef stock
2·5 ml (½ level tsp) dried marjoram
450 g (1 lb) potatoes, peeled and sliced
25 g (1 oz) stuffed green olives, sliced
4 tomatoes, skinned and quartered

Cut the lamb into 4-cm (1½-in) cubes and toss in seasoned flour. Heat the oil in a frying pan and fry the meat for 10 minutes until browned. Place in the electric casserole. Add the garlic, green pepper and celery to the pan and fry for 5 minutes. Add the stock and marjoram and bring to the boil. Pour over the meat and stir well. Add the potatoes to the casserole. Place the lid in position and cook on high for 3–4 hours or low for 6–8 hours.

Just before serving stir in the olives and tomato quarters.

Freeze without the stuffed olives and tomatoes

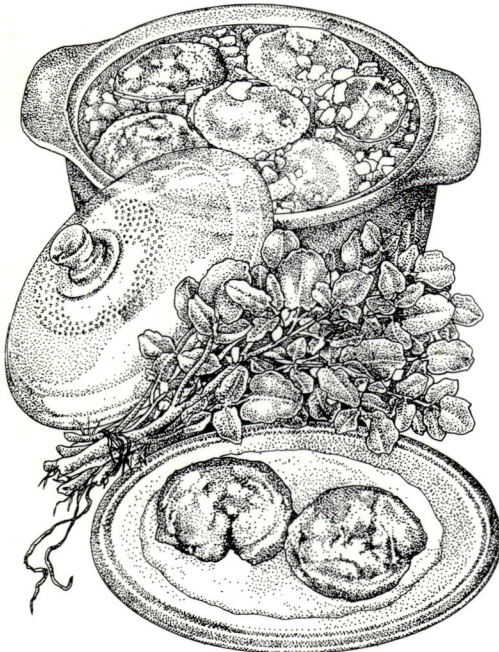

Lamb noisettes in sherry sauce

Boeuf bourguignonne (see page 65), Baked apricot trifle (see page 87)

Raisin stuffed beef rolls

A variation of beef olives, cooked on a base of apples and carrots

six 100 g (4 oz) thin slices of braising steak
30 ml (2 tbsp) vegetable oil
225 g (8 oz) carrots, peeled
225 g (8 oz) cooking apples, peeled and sliced
300 ml (½ pint) beef stock
salt and freshly ground pepper
25 g (1 oz) flour

For the stuffing
50 g (2 oz) long grain rice, cooked
50 g (2 oz) seedless raisins
grated rind of ½ lemon
30 ml (2 tbsp) freshly chopped parsley
salt and freshly ground pepper
1 egg, beaten

Trim the meat and beat out to an even thickness.

To make the stuffing: stir all the stuffing ingredients together and bind with beaten egg. Spread the stuffing over the meat slices, roll up and tie with string.

Heat the oil in a frying pan, coat the rolls in flour and brown for 10 minutes. Remove from the pan and reserve. Add the carrots and apples to the pan and fry for 5 minutes. Add the stock and seasoning and bring to the boil. Pour into the electric casserole, place the beef rolls on top and spoon over some of the stock. Place the lid in position and cook on high for 3–4 hours or low for 6–8 hours. Remove the string and serve with the vegetables and gravy.

SERVES 6

✢ Beef flamenco

15 ml (1 tbsp) vegetable oil
2 large onions, skinned and chopped
2 rashers of streaky bacon, rinded and chopped
325 g (12 oz) potatoes, peeled
700 g (1½ lb) braising steak
25 g (1 oz) flour
400 ml (¾ pint) beef stock
396-g (14-oz) can tomatoes
30 ml (2 tbsp) Worcestershire sauce
salt and freshly ground pepper
8 stuffed olives, halved

Heat the oil in a frying pan and cook the onions

and bacon for 2–3 minutes. Cut the potatoes into 1-cm (½-in) cubes, add to the pan and cook for 2–3 minutes. Place in the electric casserole. Cut the beef into 2·5-cm (1-in) cubes, add to the frying pan and fry for 10 minutes until browned. Place in the electric casserole. Stir the flour into the frying pan and cook for 1 minute. Gradually stir in the stock, tomatoes, Worcestershire sauce, seasoning and olives and bring to the boil. Pour into the electric casserole and stir well. Place the lid in position and cook on high for 3–4 hours or on low for 6–8 hours.

Freeze without the olives

✢ Boeuf bourguignonne

ILLUSTRATED IN COLOUR FACING PAGE 64

900 g (2 lb) chuck steak
salt and freshly ground pepper
45 ml (3 level tbsp) flour
30 ml (2 tbsp) vegetable oil
100-g (4-oz) piece of streaky bacon, rinded and diced
100 g (4 oz) shallots or baby onions, skinned
1 clove of garlic, skinned and crushed
100 g (4 oz) button mushrooms
300 ml (½ pint) beef stock
150 ml (¼ pint) red wine
30 ml (2 level tbsp) tomato paste
2·5 ml (½ level tsp) dried thyme
1 bayleaf
croûtons of fried bread and watercress to garnish

Cut the meat into 2·5-cm (1-in) cubes and toss in seasoned flour. Heat the oil in a frying pan, add the meat and bacon and fry for 10 minutes until browned. Place in the electric casserole. Cut a cross in the base of each onion to prevent the centre from popping out during cooking. Add the onions and garlic to the pan and cook for 5 minutes until soft. Add the mushrooms and cook for 1 minute. Stir in the stock, wine, tomato paste and herbs. Season well. Bring to the boil, stirring, pour over the beef and stir well. Place the lid in position and cook on high for 3–4 hours or low for 6–8 hours. Remove the bayleaf and garnish with watercress and croûtons.

SERVES 6

Summer berries in wine with shortbread fingers (see page 89), Orange fudge pudding (see page 83), Crème caramel (see page 89)

❖ Boeuf stroganoff

A classic dish specially adapted for the electric casserole. Just as good, but cheaper. Serve with freshly boiled rice and buttered courgette slices

45 ml (3 tbsp) vegetable oil
2 large onions, skinned and sliced
700 g (1½ lb) stewing steak, cut into strips
salt and freshly ground pepper
30 ml (2 level tbsp) flour
300 ml (½ pint) beef stock
30 ml (2 level tbsp) tomato paste
225 g (8 oz) mushrooms, thickly sliced
142-ml (5-fl oz) carton soured cream

Heat the oil in a frying pan and cook the onions for 5 minutes until soft. Place in the electric casserole. Toss the meat in seasoned flour, add to the pan and fry for 10 minutes until browned. Gradually add the stock and tomato paste and bring to the boil, stirring. Stir in the mushrooms and seasoning. Pour into the electric casserole and stir well. Place the lid in position and cook on high for 3–4 hours or low for 6–8 hours.

Just before serving stir in the soured cream.
Freeze without the soured cream

❖ Beef and apple curry

Serve with a refreshing cucumber raita, a dressed onion and tomato salad, toasted coconut and slices of banana for an extra special dinner party

900 g (2 lb) chuck steak
salt and freshly ground pepper
15 ml (1 level tbsp) flour
45 ml (3 tbsp) vegetable oil
2 large onions, skinned and chopped
225 g (8 oz) cooking apples, peeled, cored and
    chopped
1·25 ml (¼ level tsp) chilli powder
2·5 ml (½ level tsp) ground ginger
2·5 ml (½ level tsp) ground coriander
2·5 ml (½ level tsp) turmeric
2·5 ml (½ level tsp) ground cardamom
25 g (1 oz) sultanas
300 ml (½ pint) beef stock
15 ml (1 level tbsp) tomato paste

Cut the meat into 2·5-cm (1-in) cubes and toss in seasoned flour. Heat the oil in a saucepan and cook the onion and apple for 5 minutes until

soft. Place in the electric casserole. Add the meat to the pan and fry for 10 minutes until brown. Stir in the spices and sultanas and cook for 1 minute. Gradually stir in the stock and tomato paste, bring to the boil and pour into the electric casserole. Stir well. Place the lid in position and cook on high for 3–4 hours or low for 6–8 hours.
SERVES 6

❖ Beef with ale and orange

Serve with Brussels sprouts and lyonnaise pot-atoes (potatoes sautéed with onion slices)

1 kg (2¼ lb) chuck steak
30 ml (2 tbsp) vegetable oil
1 large onion, skinned and chopped
30 ml (2 level tbsp) flour
finely grated rind and juice of 1 orange
300 ml (½ pint) pale ale
15 ml (1 tbsp) redcurrant jelly
15 ml (1 level tbsp) tomato paste
salt and freshly ground pepper

Cut the meat into 5-cm (2-in) cubes. Heat the oil and fry the meat for 10 minutes until golden brown. Remove from the pan and place in the electric casserole. Add the onion to the pan and cook for 5 minutes until soft. Stir in the flour and cook for 1 minute. Add the orange rind and juice and beer and bring to the boil. Stir in the redcurrant jelly, tomato paste and seasoning. Pour over the meat in the electric casserole and stir well. Place the lid in position and cook on high for 3–4 hours or low for 6–8 hours.
SERVES 6

Braised beef steaks with celery

50 g (2 oz) red kidney beans, soaked overnight
25 g (1 oz) lard or dripping
four 125-g (4-oz) pieces braising steak
4 sticks of celery, washed and trimmed
1 medium-sized onion, skinned and sliced
400 ml (¾ pint) beef stock
30 ml (2 tbsp) sherry
salt and freshly ground pepper
15 ml (1 level tbsp) cornflour

Soak the kidney beans overnight and drain. Heat the fat in a frying pan, add the meat and fry for 10 minutes until browned on both sides. Place in the electric casserole. Cut the celery into 5-cm (2-in) lengths, add to the pan with the onions and cook for 5 minutes. Stir in the beans, stock, sherry and seasoning and bring to the boil. Pour into the electric casserole, place the lid in position and cook on high for 4–5 hours or low for 8–10 hours.

15 minutes before the end of cooking time blend the cornflour to a smooth paste with a little water. Stir into the casserole, replace the lid and cook until the sauce thickens.

Beef olives

Serve with herb-flavoured rice and buttered baby carrots for a special party meal

8 thin slices topside of beef
salt and freshly ground pepper
45 ml (3 level tbsp) flour
30 ml (2 tbsp) vegetable oil
2 medium-sized onions, skinned and sliced
600 ml (1 pint) beef stock
15 ml (1 level tbsp) tomato paste

For the stuffing
25 g (1 oz) butter
50 g (2 oz) bacon, rinded and chopped
50 g (2 oz) flat mushrooms, chopped
50 g (2 oz) shredded suet
50 g (2 oz) fresh white breadcrumbs
15 ml (1 tbsp) freshly chopped parsley
1 egg, beaten

To make the stuffing: melt the butter in a pan and fry the bacon and mushrooms for 8–10 minutes until golden brown. Stir in the remaining ingredients except the egg; add enough egg to bind. Spread the stuffing on the meat slices and roll up. Secure with string and toss in seasoned flour.

Heat the oil in a frying pan and fry the beef rolls for 5 minutes until lightly browned on all sides. Remove from the pan and place in the electric casserole. Add the onion slices to the pan, cook for 5 minutes and place in the electric casserole with the beef olives. Add the remaining flour to the pan and cook for 1 minute. Stir in

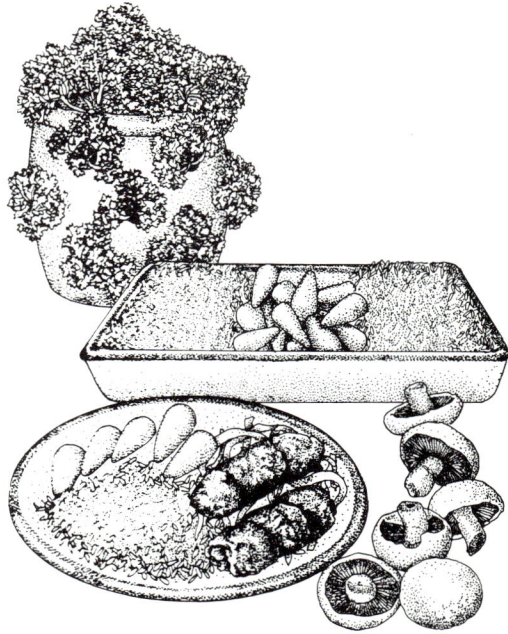

Beef olives

the stock and tomato paste and bring to the boil. Pour over the beef olives and place the lid in position. Cook on high for 3–4 hours or low for 6–8 hours. Remove the string before serving.

Sweet and sour casserole

60 ml (4 tbsp) vegetable oil
1 large onion, skinned and chopped
100 g (4 oz) carrots, peeled and cut into strips
275 g (10 oz) white cabbage, shredded
salt and freshly ground pepper
700 g (1½ lb) chuck steak
30 ml (2 level tbsp) flour
400 ml (¾ pint) beef stock
30 ml (2 level tbsp) soft brown sugar
15 ml (1 tbsp) soy sauce
150 ml (¼ pint) white wine
30 ml (2 level tbsp) tomato paste
226-g (8-oz) can tomatoes
freshly chopped parsley to garnish

Heat half the oil in a pan, add the onion, carrots and cabbage, cook for 5 minutes until soft and place in the electric casserole. Cut the meat into 2·5-cm (1-in) cubes. Season well. Add the remaining oil to the pan and cook the meat for 10 minutes until golden brown. Remove and place in the electric casserole. Stir in the flour and cook for 1 minute. Heat the stock and then dissolve the sugar with the soy sauce in the hot stock. Add to the pan with the wine, tomato paste and tomatoes and bring to the boil. Pour into the electric casserole and stir well. Place the lid in position and cook on high for 3–4 hours or low for 6–8 hours. Serve sprinkled with chopped parsley.

✤ Beef and liver pâté

225 g (8 oz) chicken livers, washed
2–3 sticks of celery, washed and chopped
1 small onion, skinned and chopped
2 cloves of garlic, skinned and crushed
25 g (1 oz) walnuts, finely chopped
10 ml (2 level tsp) salt
freshly ground black pepper
2·5 ml (½ level tsp) dried thyme
2·5 ml (½ level tsp) ground nutmeg
2 eggs, beaten
30 ml (2 tbsp) single cream
450 g (1 lb) minced beef
100 g (4 oz) streaky bacon, rinded

Trim the liver and chop finely. Purée in a blender with all the other ingredients except the minced beef and streaky bacon, until smooth. Stir in the minced beef. Line a 1·1-litre (2-pint) soufflé or ovenproof dish with the bacon. Turn the pâté

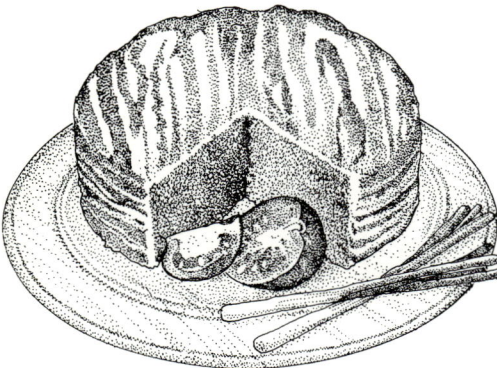

Beef and liver pâté

mixture into the dish and press down well. Cover tightly with foil and place in the electric casserole with boiling water to come halfway up the dish. Place the lid in position and cook on high for 2–3 hours or low for 4–6 hours.

Remove the dish from the electric casserole. Leave to cool under weights – place a saucer on top of the pâté and stand a can on top of it.

✤ Beef braised in red wine

Serve with duchesse potatoes browned under the grill and grilled tomatoes

700 g (1½ lb) braising steak
50 g (2 oz) flour
salt and freshly ground pepper
30 ml (2 tbsp) vegetable oil
1 leek, sliced and washed
225 g (8 oz) carrots, peeled and sliced
1 clove of garlic, skinned and crushed
15 ml (1 tbsp) freshly chopped parsley
15 ml (1 tbsp) freshly chopped chives
30 ml (2 tbsp) brandy
150 ml (¼ pint) red wine
150 ml (¼ pint) beef stock

Cut the beef into 3·5-cm (1½-in) cubes and toss in seasoned flour. Heat the oil in a frying pan and fry the meat for 10 minutes until browned. Place in the electric casserole. Add the vegetables to the pan and cook for 5 minutes. Stir in the remaining ingredients and bring to the boil, stirring. Pour into the electric casserole and stir well. Place the lid in position and cook on high for 3–4 hours or low for 6–8 hours.

✤ Turkey paprika with pasta

30 ml (2 tbsp) vegetable oil
1 large onion, skinned and finely sliced
700 g (1½ lb) turkey breasts, skinned
15 ml (1 level tbsp) paprika
400 ml (¾ pint) chicken stock
15 ml (1 level tbsp) tomato paste
1 red pepper, seeded and chopped
salt and freshly ground pepper
100 g (4 oz) pasta shapes
15 ml (1 level tbsp) cornflour
freshly chopped parsley
60 ml (4 tbsp) soured cream

Heat the oil in a frying pan and fry the onion for 5 minutes. Place in the electric casserole. Cut the turkey into finger-size pieces. Add to the pan and fry for 5 minutes. Place in the electric casserole. Stir the paprika into the pan and cook for 1 minute. Gradually stir in the stock, tomato paste, pepper and seasoning and bring to the boil. Pour over the onions and turkey in the electric casserole and stir well. Place the lid in position and cook on high for 2–3 hours or low for 4–6 hours.

45 minutes before the end of cooking time turn the electric casserole to high. Stir in the pasta shapes, replace the lid and continue cooking.

Just before serving blend the cornflour to a smooth paste with a little cold water and stir into the casserole. Serve garnished with parsley and a swirl of soured cream.

SERVES 6

Freeze without the parsley and soured cream

✢ Turkey in mushroom cream sauce

Turkey meat goes a long way because there is very little wastage. It's a good buy in most supermarkets all the year round

700 g (1½ lb) turkey breasts
salt and freshly ground pepper
25 g (1 oz) flour
50 g (2 oz) butter
1 medium-sized onion, skinned and chopped
100 g (4 oz) button mushrooms
300 ml (½ pint) chicken stock
150 ml (¼ pint) white wine
salt and freshly ground pepper
50 g (2 oz) cooked ham, chopped
142-ml (5-fl oz) carton double cream
30 ml (2 tbsp) brandy
30 ml (2 tbsp) freshly chopped parsley

Cut the turkey breasts in half lengthways and beat out to an even thickness with a rolling pin. Toss in seasoned flour. Melt the butter in a frying pan and fry the turkey for 1 minute on each side. Remove from the pan and reserve. Add the onion and mushrooms to the pan and fry for 3–4 minutes. Add the stock, wine and seasoning and bring to the boil. Pour into the

electric casserole and add the turkey. Place the lid in position and cook on high for 2–3 hours or low for 4–6 hours.

15 minutes before serving stir in the ham, cream, brandy and parsley, replace the lid and continue cooking.

SERVES 6

Freeze without the ham, cream, brandy and parsley

✢ Creamed chicken with ginger and celery

A complete meal for any occasion. Just serve with hot garlic bread

40 g (1½ oz) flour
15 ml (1 level tbsp) paprika
salt and freshly ground pepper
2·5 ml (1 level tsp) ground ginger
4 chicken portions, skinned
50 g (2 oz) butter
15 ml (1 tbsp) vegetable oil
1 medium-sized onion, skinned and chopped
4 sticks of celery, washed and chopped
225 g (8 oz) button mushrooms
225 g (8 oz) tomatoes, skinned and chopped
400 ml (¾ pint) chicken stock
150 ml (¼ pint) white wine
175 g (6 oz) spaghetti, broken up
142-ml (5-fl oz) carton soured cream
freshly chopped chives

Stir the flour, paprika, seasoning and ginger together and coat the chicken with the mixture. Melt the butter and oil in a large frying pan and fry the chicken for 10 minutes until golden brown. Remove from the pan and place in the electric casserole. Fry the onion, celery, mushrooms and tomatoes for 2–3 minutes, add the stock and wine and bring to the boil. Pour into the electric casserole. Place the lid in position and cook on high for 3–4 hours or low for 6–8 hours.

45 minutes before the end of cooking time, turn the electric casserole to high, add the broken pieces of spaghetti, replace the lid and continue cooking. Just before serving, stir the soured cream into the casserole and sprinkle with the chives.

Freeze without the spaghetti and soured cream

Roast chicken with bacon stuffing balls

Roast chicken with bacon stuffing balls

A whole chicken 'roasted' in the electric casserole with mushroom and bacon stuffing balls

50 g (2 oz) butter or margarine
1·4–1·8-kg (3–4-lb) oven ready chicken
150 ml (¼ pint) chicken stock
15 ml (1 level tbsp) cornflour

For the stuffing
225 g (8 oz) streaky bacon, rinded and chopped
100 g (4 oz) mushrooms, chopped
100 g (4 oz) fresh white breadcrumbs
30 ml (2 tbsp) freshly chopped parsley
salt and freshly ground pepper
1 egg, beaten

Grease the inside of the electric casserole with 25 g (1 oz) of the fat. Wipe the chicken inside and out with paper towel and season well. Melt the remaining fat in a frying pan and fry the chicken for 10 minutes until browned all over. Place in the electric casserole.

To make the stuffing: stir the stuffing ingredients together and bind with egg. Shape into twelve small balls. Add to the frying pan and cook for 5 minutes until browned. Place in the electric casserole. Place the lid in position and cook on high for 3–4 hours.

15 minutes before the end of cooking lift the chicken and stuffing from the casserole, place on a heated serving dish and keep warm. Stir the stock and cornflour together, add to the casserole, replace the lid and continue cooking. Serve the sauce separately.
SERVES 6

✣ Chicken Burgundy casserole

Serve this tasty rich casserole with fried triangles of bread; garnish with freshly chopped parsley

30 ml (2 tbsp) vegetable oil
25 g (1 oz) butter
4 chicken portions, skinned
1 medium-sized onion, skinned and chopped
50 g (2 oz) streaky bacon, rinded and chopped
25 g (1 oz) flour
150 ml (¼ pint) dry red wine (Burgundy)
100 g (4 oz) button mushrooms
salt and freshly ground pepper
bouquet garni

Heat the oil and butter in a frying pan, add the chicken and cook for 10 minutes until golden brown. Place in the electric casserole. Add the onion and bacon to the frying pan and cook for 5 minutes until soft. Stir in the flour and cook for 1 minute. Gradually stir in the wine, mushrooms and seasoning and bring to the boil, stirring. Pour over the chicken in the electric casserole and add the bouquet garni. Place the lid in position and cook on high for 3–4 hours or on low for 6–8 hours. Remove the bouquet garni before serving or freezing.

✣ Cider cream chicken

50 g (2 oz) butter
1½-kg (3-lb) roasting chicken, washed
1 medium-sized onion, skinned and chopped
3 sticks of celery, washed and chopped
45 ml (3 level tbsp) flour
150 ml (¼ pint) dry cider
300 ml (½ pint) chicken stock
325 g (12 oz) cooking apples, peeled, cored and chopped
salt and freshly ground pepper
142-ml (5-fl oz) carton double cream

Melt the butter in a frying pan and cook the

chicken for 10 minutes until browned. Place in the electric casserole. Add the onion and celery to the frying pan and cook for 5 minutes until soft. Stir in the flour and cook for 1 minute. Gradually stir in the cider, stock, apples and seasoning. Bring to the boil, stirring, and pour over the chicken in the electric casserole. Place the lid in position and cook on high for 3–4 hours or on low for 6–8 hours.

10 minutes before the end of cooking time transfer the chicken to a serving dish and keep warm. Skim the excess fat from the sauce and stir in the cream. Replace the lid and continue cooking.

To serve, carve the chicken and pour the sauce over it.

Carve the chicken before freezing. Freeze without the cream

✢ Spiced chicken with cashew nuts

Serve with sauté potatoes and petits pois

30 ml (2 tbsp) vegetable oil
2 large onions, skinned and finely chopped
2 cloves of garlic, skinned and crushed
4 chicken portions, skinned
15 ml (1 level tbsp) flour
salt and freshly ground pepper
15 ml (1 level tbsp) curry powder
5 ml (1 level tsp) chilli powder
300 ml (½ pint) chicken stock
15 ml (1 level tbsp) cornflour
100 g (4 oz) cashew nuts
two 141-g (5-oz) cartons yogurt

Heat the oil in a frying pan, add the onions and garlic and cook for 5 minutes until soft. Place in the electric casserole. Add the chicken to the pan and cook for 10 minutes until golden brown. Place in the electric casserole. Stir the flour, seasoning and spices into the pan juices and cook for 1 minute. Gradually stir in the stock, and bring to the boil, stirring. Pour over the chicken. Place the lid in position and cook on high for 3–4 hours or low for 6–8 hours.

30 minutes before the end of cooking time blend the cornflour to a smooth paste with a little water and stir into the electric casserole

with the nuts and yogurt. Replace the lid and continue cooking.

Freeze without the cashew nuts and yogurt

✢ Neapolitan chicken

A colourful chicken casserole. Serve with sautéed courgettes and buttered noodles

4 chicken portions, skinned
60 ml (4 tbsp) vegetable oil
2 medium-sized onions, skinned and sliced
1 small red pepper, seeded and sliced
45 ml (3 level tbsp) flour
150 ml (¼ pint) red wine
396-g (14-oz) can tomatoes
5 ml (1 level tsp) dried marjoram
5 ml (1 level tsp) salt
freshly ground black pepper
6 black olives, stoned and halved

Trim and wipe the chicken portions. Heat the oil in a frying pan and fry the chicken for 10 minutes until golden brown. Place in the electric casserole. Add the onions to the pan and cook for 5 minutes until soft. Add the pepper and continue cooking for 5 minutes until the onion is golden brown. Stir in the flour and cook for 1 minute. Gradually stir in the wine, tomatoes, marjoram and seasoning. Bring to the boil, stirring. Add the olives and pour over the chicken in the electric casserole. Place the lid in position and cook on high for 3–4 hours or on low for 6–8 hours.

Freeze without the olives

Chicken ratatouille

Serve with buttered noodles or pasta shells

4 chicken breasts
8 rashers streaky bacon, rinded
15 ml (1 tbsp) vegetable oil
1 onion, skinned and sliced
2 courgettes, sliced
2 large tomatoes, skinned and sliced
1 aubergine, sliced
15 ml (1 level tbsp) flour
600 ml (1 pint) chicken stock
15 ml (1 level tbsp) tomato paste
salt and freshly ground pepper
2·5 ml (½ level tsp) dried mixed herbs

Remove the skin from the chicken breasts and wrap two pieces of bacon around each joint. Heat the oil in a frying pan and fry the bacon-wrapped chicken for 10 minutes on each side until golden brown. Remove from the pan, drain on kitchen paper towel and reserve. Add the onion and courgettes to the pan and fry for 5 minutes until soft. Add the tomatoes and aubergine to the pan and continue frying for a further 5 minutes. Remove from the pan and place in the electric casserole. Place the chicken on top. Mix the flour with the remaining oil in the pan and gradually add the stock. Bring to the boil, add the tomato paste, seasoning and herbs. Pour over the chicken in the electric casserole. Place the lid in position and cook on high for 3–4 hours or low for 6–8 hours.

✢ Tarragon chicken in white wine

Serve with potato croquettes and chopped spinach

4 chicken portions
50 g (2 oz) flour
15 ml (1 tbsp) vegetable oil
25 g (1 oz) butter
1 small onion, skinned and chopped
1 stick of celery, washed and chopped
1 clove of garlic, skinned and crushed
400 ml (¾ pint) chicken stock
150 ml (¼ pint) white wine
5 ml (1 level tsp) dried tarragon
salt and freshly ground pepper
142-ml (5-fl oz) carton double cream
freshly chopped parsley

Wash and skin the chicken portions and toss in 25 g (1 oz) of the flour. Heat the oil and butter in a frying pan and fry the chicken for 10 minutes until golden brown. Remove and place in the electric casserole. Add the onion, celery and garlic to the pan and cook for 1 minute. Stir in the remaining flour and then gradually stir in the stock. Bring to the boil, add the white wine, tarragon and seasoning, then pour over the chicken in the electric casserole. Place the lid in position and cook on high for 3–4 hours or low for 6–8 hours.

Just before serving stir in the cream and sprinkle with freshly chopped parsley.
Freeze without the cream

✢ Duck in red wine sauce

Serve with new potatoes and fresh garden peas

15 g (½ oz) butter
1 duck about 2–2¼ kg (4–4½ lb), skinned and quartered
1 large onion, skinned and sliced
225 g (8 oz) button mushrooms
30 ml (2 level tbsp) flour
300 ml (½ pint) red wine
150 ml (¼ pint) chicken stock
salt and freshly ground pepper
15 ml (1 level tbsp) tomato paste
25 g (1 oz) flaked almonds, toasted

Melt the butter in a frying pan and fry the duck for 10 minutes, until well browned. Drain on paper towel to remove excess fat and place in the electric casserole. Add the onion and mushrooms to the pan and cook for 5 minutes until soft. Stir in the flour and cook for a further minute. Gradually stir in the wine, stock, seasoning and tomato paste and bring to the boil. Pour over the duck in the electric casserole. Place the lid in position and cook on high for 4–5 hours or low for 8–10 hours.

Just before serving skim off all the excess fat. Serve with almonds sprinkled over the top.
Freeze without the flaked almonds

Pheasant casseroled in port and orange

Check that the cleaned pheasants will fit into your electric casserole. If they are a little large, chop each in half lengthways

two small pheasants, cleaned
30 ml (2 tbsp) vegetable oil
300 ml (½ pint) chicken stock
120 ml (8 tbsp) port
finely grated rind and juice of 2 oranges
50 g (2 oz) sultanas
salt and freshly ground pepper
15 ml (1 level tbsp) cornflour
25 g (1 oz) flaked almonds, toasted

Wipe the pheasants with kitchen paper towel. Heat the oil in a frying pan and fry the pheasants for 10 minutes until browned all over. Place in the electric casserole. Add the stock, port, orange rind and juice, sultanas and seasoning to the pan and bring to the boil. Pour over the pheasants. Place the lid in position and cook on high for 4–5 hours or low for 8–10 hours.

Just before serving blend the cornflour to a smooth paste with a little cold water and stir into the juices. Replace the lid and continue cooking. Serve the pheasants with the sauce spooned over them and garnished with almonds.

Pork fillet with mustard cream

A subtle blend of apple, mustard, mushrooms and soured cream. Serve with boiled rice and follow with a green salad

450 g (1 lb) pork fillet (tenderloin)
salt and freshly ground black pepper
30 ml (2 level tbsp) flour
50 g (2 oz) butter
1 medium-sized onion, skinned and chopped
225 g (8 oz) mushrooms, sliced
1 large cooking apple, peeled, cored and chopped
150 ml (¼ pint) chicken stock
15 ml (1 level tbsp) Meaux or French mustard
142-ml (5-fl oz) carton soured cream
freshly chopped parsley

Cut the pork into thin strips and toss in seasoned flour. Melt half the butter in a frying pan, add the onion and cook for 5 minutes until soft. Add the mushrooms and apple and cook for 2–3 minutes. Place in the electric casserole. Melt the remaining butter in the frying pan, add the meat and fry for 10 minutes until browned. Stir in the stock and mustard. Season and bring to the boil. Pour into the electric casserole and stir well. Place the lid in position and cook on high for 3–4 hours or low for 6–8 hours.

5 minutes before the end of cooking time stir in the soured cream. Serve garnished with parsley.

Pork and apple in red wine

Serve with leaf spinach and creamed potatoes

700 g (1½ lb) pork spare rib chops, cut into 2·5-cm (1-in) strips
salt and freshly ground pepper
25 g (1 oz) flour
15 ml (1 tbsp) vegetable oil
25 g (1 oz) butter
1 medium-sized onion, skinned and chopped
2 rashers streaky bacon, rinded and chopped
1 green pepper, seeded and sliced
150 ml (¼ pint) red wine
400 ml (¾ pint) chicken stock
1 bay leaf
1·25 ml (¼ level tsp) dried basil
2 large cooking apples, peeled, cored and chopped
100 g (4 oz) button mushrooms
freshly chopped parsley

Toss the pork strips in seasoned flour. Heat the oil and butter in a frying pan, cook the pork for 10 minutes until golden brown and place in the electric casserole. Add the onion, bacon and pepper to the frying pan and cook for 5 minutes until soft. Stir in the wine and stock and bring to the boil. Add the herbs, apple, mushrooms and seasoning, bring back to the boil and pour into the electric casserole. Stir well. Place the lid in position and cook on high for 3–4 hours or low for 6–8 hours. Remove the bayleaf. Serve garnished with parsley.
SERVES 6

Cidered pot roast pork

Serve with duchesse potatoes and buttered carrots

1·4-kg (3-lb) pork leg joint
15 ml (1 tbsp) vegetable oil
2 large cooking apples, peeled
150 ml (¼ pint) dry cider
150 ml (¼ pint) chicken stock
15 ml (1 level tbsp) demerara sugar
10 ml (2 level tsp) ground ginger
salt and freshly ground pepper
15 ml (1 level tbsp) cornflour

Trim the skin and fat from the pork. Heat the oil in a frying pan and cook the joint for 10 minutes until browned on all sides. Remove from the pan and reserve. Cut the apples into quarters, remove the cores and cook in the pan for 1 minute. Add the cider and stock and bring to the boil. Pour into the electric casserole and place the pork on top. Spoon the sugar, ginger and seasoning over the pork. Place the lid in position and cook on high for 4–5 hours.

10 minutes before the end of the cooking time place the pork on a heated serving dish and keep warm. Blend the cornflour to a smooth paste with a little cold water, stir into the sauce, replace the lid and cook until thickened. Slice the pork and serve the sauce separately.

SERVES 6

Cidered pot roast pork (see page 73)

Pork fillet with sage stuffing

Serve with a tossed green salad and boiled new potatoes

two 350-g (12-oz) pork fillets
25 g (1 oz) flour
salt and freshly ground pepper
25 g (1 oz) butter
100 g (4 oz) button mushrooms
150 ml (¼ pint) dry white wine
150 ml (¼ pint) chicken stock
60 ml (4 tbsp) soured cream
freshly chopped parsley

For the stuffing
25 g (1 oz) butter
1 small onion, skinned and finely chopped
225 g (8 oz) streaky bacon, rinded and finely chopped
100 g (4 oz) fresh white breadcrumbs
30 ml (2 tbsp) freshly chopped sage
30 ml (2 tbsp) freshly chopped parsley
salt and freshly ground pepper
1 egg, beaten

Make a vertical cut in each fillet, along its length and two thirds of the way through. Open the fillets out, cover with greaseproof paper and beat to an even thickness with a rolling pin. Coat in seasoned flour.

To make the stuffing: melt the butter in a saucepan, add the onion and bacon and cook for 5 minutes. Stir in the remaining ingredients.

Spread the stuffing over the fillets, roll up and tie neatly with string.

Melt the butter in a frying pan and fry the fillet rolls for 10 minutes until evenly browned. Place them in the electric casserole with the mushrooms, wine, stock and seasoning. Place the lid in position and cook on high for 4–5 hours or low for 8–10 hours.

Take the fillets from the casserole and remove the strings. Stir the cream and parsley into the casserole and pour the sauce over the pork fillets. Cut each fillet in half to serve.

✤ Veal fricassee

Serve with broccoli and potato croquettes

1¼ kg (2½ lb) stewing veal
50 g (2 oz) butter
225 g (8 oz) bacon, rinded and chopped
2 large onions, skinned and sliced
45 ml (3 level tbsp) flour
400 ml (¾ pint) chicken or veal stock
150 ml (¼ pint) dry white wine
2·5 ml (½ level tsp) dried marjoram
salt and freshly ground black pepper
100 g (4 oz) button mushrooms
142-ml (5-fl oz) carton single cream
freshly chopped parsley

Cut the veal into 2-cm (¾-in) cubes. Melt half the butter in a frying pan, add the veal and bacon and cook for 5 minutes without browning. Place in the electric casserole. Melt the remaining butter in the frying pan, add the onions and cook for 5 minutes until soft. Stir in the flour and cook for 1 minute. Gradually stir in the stock, wine, marjoram and seasoning. Bring to the boil, stirring. Pour into the electric casserole with the mushrooms and stir well. Place the lid in position and cook on high for 3–4 hours or low for 6–8 hours.

15 minutes before the end of cooking time stir in the cream, replace the lid and continue cooking. Serve garnished with parsley.

Freeze without the cream

✤ Veal goulash with caraway dumplings

For a simple supper party serve the goulash with French bread

30 ml (2 tbsp) vegetable oil
700 g (1½ lb) pie veal, cubed
1 large onion, skinned and sliced
1 large green pepper, seeded and sliced
30 ml (2 level tbsp) paprika
30 ml (2 level tbsp) flour
226-g (8-oz) can tomatoes
300 ml (½ pint) chicken stock
salt and freshly ground pepper
pinch of ground nutmeg
1·25 ml (¼ level tsp) dried sage

For the dumplings
100 g (4 oz) self raising flour
50 g (2 oz) shredded suet
2·5 ml (½ level tsp) caraway seeds
1·25 ml (¼ level tsp) salt

Heat the oil in a frying pan and cook the meat for 10 minutes until browned. Place in the electric casserole. Add the onion and pepper to the pan and cook for 5–10 minutes until beginning to brown. Add the paprika and flour and cook for 1 minute. Add the tomatoes, stock, seasoning and herbs and bring to the boil, stirring. Pour over the meat in the electric casserole and stir well. Place lid in position and cook on high of 3–4 hours or low for 6–8 hours.

To make the dumplings: stir the dry ingredients together with enough cold water to mix to a soft dough and shape into eight even sized balls.

45 minutes before the end of cooking time, turn the electric casserole to high. Add the dumplings to the electric casserole, pushing under the surface. Replace the lid and continue cooking.

Freeze without the dumplings

✤ Blanquette of veal

A rich creamy sauce provides the distinctive flavour of this classic dish and the electric casserole is a perfect way of gently simmering the veal. A green salad makes a good contrast

700 g (1½ lb) boned leg of veal, trimmed
15 ml (1 tbsp) vegetable oil
8 button onions, skinned
450 g (1 lb) small new carrots, scraped
1 bayleaf
1·25 ml (¼ level tsp) dried thyme
salt and freshly ground pepper
400 ml (¾ pint) chicken stock
freshly chopped parsley

For the sauce
25 g (1 oz) butter
25 g (1 oz) flour
150 ml (¼ pint) milk
60 ml (4 tbsp) double cream
15 ml (1 tbsp) lemon juice

Cut the veal into 2·5-cm (1-in) cubes. Heat the oil in a frying pan. Fry the veal for 5 minutes. Place in the electric casserole. Add the vegetables, herbs, seasoning and stock to the pan and bring to the boil. Pour into the electric casserole and stir well. Place the lid in position and cook on high for 3–4 hours or low for 6–8 hours.

20 minutes before the end of the cooking time melt the butter in a saucepan, add the flour and cook for 1 minute. Pour in the milk, bring to the boil, stirring. Add the cream and lemon juice. Stir the sauce into the casserole, replace the lid and continue cooking. Serve sprinkled with chopped parsley.

Freeze without the cream

Bacon stuffed veal rolls

Serve with buttered noodles or boiled rice and courgettes

6 slices leg of veal
salt and freshly ground pepper
25 g (1 oz) flour
30 ml (2 tbsp) vegetable oil
225 g (8 oz) button onions, skinned
225 g (8 oz) carrots, peeled and diced
100 g (4 oz) button mushrooms
400 ml (¾ pint) chicken stock
45 ml (3 tbsp) sweet sherry
15 ml (1 level tbsp) tomato paste

For the stuffing
75 g (3 oz) streaky bacon, rinded and chopped
50 g (2 oz) shredded suet
75 g (3 oz) fresh white breadcrumbs
grated rind and juice of ½ lemon
30 ml (2 tbsp) freshly chopped parsley
1 egg, beaten

Beat out the slices of veal to an even thickness.

To make the stuffing: fry the bacon in its own fat for 5 minutes, add to the rest of the stuffing ingredients, mix together and season well. Spread the stuffing over the veal slices, roll up and tie with string. Roll in seasoned flour.

Heat the oil in a frying pan and cook the veal rolls for 10 minutes until browned. Remove from the pan and reserve. Add the vegetables to the pan and cook for 5 minutes. Stir in the stock, sherry and tomato paste. Season and bring to the boil. Pour into the electric casserole, place the veal rolls on top and spoon over a little stock. Place the lid in position and cook on high for 3–4 hours or low for 6–8 hours.

Osso bucco

Ask your butcher to prepare the veal for you

1 kg (2¼ lb) shin of veal, cut into 5-cm (2-in) pieces
salt and freshly ground pepper
50 g (2 oz) butter
1 onion, skinned and chopped
1 clove of garlic, skinned and crushed
1 carrot, peeled and sliced
2 sticks of celery, washed and chopped
15 ml (1 level tbsp) flour
400 ml (¾ pint) chicken stock
150 ml (¼ pint) white wine
225 g (8 oz) tomatoes, skinned and chopped
grated rind of ½ lemon
freshly chopped parsley

Melt the butter in a large saucepan, season the veal and cook for 10 minutes until brown. Remove from the pan and place in the electric casserole. Fry the onion, garlic, carrot and celery for 3–4 minutes. Stir in the flour and gradually add the stock and wine, tomatoes and lemon rind. Bring to the boil and pour the sauce into the electric casserole. Place the lid in position and cook on high for 3–4 hours or low for 6–8 hours. Serve sprinkled with parsley.

Puddings from the pot

Apple and coconut pudding

When the pudding is cooked, turn it out on to a heated plate and serve with hot custard sauce

For the pastry
225 g (8 oz) self raising flour
pinch of salt
100 g (4 oz) shredded suet

For the filling
1 medium-sized cooking apple, peeled, cored and sliced
75 ml (5 tbsp) golden syrup
30 ml (2 tbsp) warm water
25 g (1 oz) butter, softened
75 g (3 oz) seedless raisins
25 g (1 oz) desiccated coconut
25 g (1 oz) walnuts, chopped
2·5 ml (½ level tsp) mixed spice

To make the pastry: stir the flour, salt and suet together. Add enough water to mix to a soft dough. Turn on to a floured surface and knead gently. Roll out and use two thirds to line a greased 900-ml (1½-pint) pudding basin

To make the filling: place half the apple slices in the pudding basin. Stir the remaining ingredients together and spoon on top of the apple. Cover with remaining apple.

Place the pastry lid on the pudding and seal the edges. Cover with greased greaseproof paper and foil and secure with string. Place in the electric casserole with enough boiling water to come halfway up the basin. Place the lid in position and cook on high for 3–4 hours.

Treacle layer pudding

For the pastry
175 g (6 oz) self raising flour
pinch of salt
75 g (3 oz) shredded suet

For the filling
45 ml (3 tbsp) black treacle
25 g (1 oz) fresh white breadcrumbs
50 g (2 oz) walnuts, chopped
5 ml (1 level tsp) mixed spice

Stir the flour, salt and suet together. Add enough water to mix to a soft dough. Turn on to a floured surface; knead gently; roll into three circles, the first small enough to fit the base of a 900-ml (1½-pint) pudding basin, the other two to fit the middle and the top of the basin. Stir the treacle, breadcrumbs, nuts and mixed spice together. Spoon half the mixture onto the bottom layer of pastry, cover with the second layer, add the rest of the filling and top with the largest circle of pastry. Cover the basin with a layer of greased greaseproof paper and foil and secure with string. Place in the electric casserole with boiling water to come halfway up the basin. Place the lid in position and cook on high for 4–5 hours.

Black cap pudding

This old fashioned favourite – prune and cherry topped ginger flavoured sponge – cooks beautifully in the electric casserole

For the topping
15 g (½ oz) dark soft brown sugar
100 g (4 oz) dried prunes
6 glacé cherries
15 ml (1 tbsp) water

For the sponge
100 g (4 oz) dark soft brown sugar
100 g (4 oz) soft tub margarine
2 eggs, beaten
100 g (4 oz) self raising flour
2·5 ml (½ level tsp) ground ginger

To make the topping: spoon the sugar into a greased 900-ml (1½-pint) pudding basin. Split six prunes in half, remove the stones and replace with the glacé cherries. Arrange the stuffed prunes on top of the sugar, cover with the remaining prunes and sprinkle with water.

To make the sponge: cream the sugar and margarine together in a bowl until light and fluffy. Gradually beat in the eggs. Fold in the flour and ginger and spoon the mixture into the pudding basin. Cover with greased greaseproof paper and foil and secure with string. Place in the electric casserole with boiling water to come halfway up the basin. Place the lid in position and cook on high for 3–4 hours.

Apricot and raisin sponge pudding

For the topping
25 g (1 oz) dark soft brown sugar
100 g (4 oz) dried apricots
15 ml (1 tbsp) water

For the sponge
100 g (4 oz) dark soft brown sugar
100 g (4 oz) soft tub margarine
2 eggs, beaten
50 g (2 oz) seedless raisins
100 g (4 oz) self raising flour
2·5 ml (½ level tsp) ground nutmeg

To make the topping: spoon the sugar into a greased 900-ml (1½-pint) pudding basin. Place the apricots on top and sprinkle with the water.

To make the sponge: cream the sugar and margarine together in a bowl until light and fluffy. Gradually beat in the eggs and stir in the

Black cap pudding

raisins. Fold in the flour and nutmeg and spoon the mixture into the pudding basin. Cover with greased greaseproof paper and foil and secure with string. Place in the electric casserole with boiling water to come halfway up the side of the basin. Place the lid in position and cook on high for 3–4 hours.

Almond figgy pudding

The marzipan melts during cooking – don't mistake it for uncooked sponge

100 g (4 oz) butter or soft tub margarine
65 g (2½ oz) caster sugar
2 eggs, beaten
grated rind and juice of 1 lemon
100 g (4 oz) ready made marzipan, cut into small cubes
100 g (4 oz) self raising flour
425-g (15-oz) can figs, drained and quartered

Grease a 1·1-litre (2-pint) pudding basin. Cream the butter and sugar until pale and fluffy. Gradually beat in the eggs. Stir in the lemon rind, juice and marzipan, then fold in the sifted flour. Place a layer of figs in the bottom of the basin and cover with half the sponge mixture, repeat with remaining figs and sponge mixture. Cover with greased greaseproof paper and foil and secure with string. Place in the electric casserole with boiling water to come halfway up the basin. Place the lid in position and cook on high for 2–3 hours.

Bread pudding

For a crisp top, place the dish under a hot grill for 2–3 minutes until golden brown and sprinkle with extra sugar

225 g (8 oz) stale white bread
300 ml (½ pint) milk
175 g (6 oz) currants, sultanas or raisins
50 g (2 oz) demerara sugar
5–10 ml (1–2 tsp) mixed spice
50 g (2 oz) shredded suet
1 egg, beaten
ground nutmeg
demarara sugar for topping

Remove the crusts from the bread and crumble

into small pieces. Pour the milk over the bread and leave to soak for 30 minutes. Beat out the lumps. Add the fruit, sugar, spice and suet and mix well. Beat in the egg and extra milk, if required, to make a soft, dropping consistency. Pour into a greased 900-ml (1½-pint) ovenproof dish and sprinkle nutmeg on the top. Place in the electric casserole with boiling water to come halfway up the dish. Place the lid in position and cook on high for 4–5 hours.

Golden pudding

Serve with more golden syrup: heat it in a saucepan for a few minutes to make pouring easier

30 ml (2 tbsp) golden syrup
75 g (3 oz) self raising flour
75 g (3 oz) fresh white breadcrumbs
75 g (3 oz) shredded suet
pinch of salt
50 g (2 oz) caster sugar
finely grated rind of ½ lemon
about 150 ml (¼ pint) milk

Spoon the golden syrup into a greased 900-ml (1½-pint) pudding basin. Stir the flour, bread-crumbs, suet, salt, sugar and lemon rind to-gether in a mixing bowl. Stir in enough milk to mix to a soft dropping consistency. Turn the mixture into the basin, cover with greased greaseproof paper and foil and secure with string. Place in the electric casserole with boiling water to come halfway up the basin. Place the lid in position and cook on high for 3–4 hours.

Spotted Dick

175 g (6 oz) self raising flour
75 g (3 oz) fresh white breadcrumbs
100 g (4 oz) shredded suet
75 g (3 oz) caster sugar
75 g (3 oz) currants
about 200 ml (7 fl oz) milk

Mix the dry ingredients together and add enough milk to mix to a soft dough. Place in a well greased 900-ml (1½-pint) pudding basin.

Cover with greased greaseproof paper and foil and secure with string. Place in the electric casserole with boiling water to come halfway up the basin. Place the lid in position and cook on high for 3–4 hours.

✤ Chocolate orange sponge pudding

Stir the grated rind and juice of 1 orange into 600 ml (1 pint) custard to make a quick orange sauce to serve with this dish

150 g (5 oz) self raising flour
45 ml (3 level tbsp) cocoa powder
1 medium-sized orange
100 g (4 oz) soft tub margarine
100 g (4 oz) caster sugar
2 eggs, beaten
milk to mix

Sift the flour and cocoa together into a mixing bowl and grate in the orange rind. Cut all the peel and pith from the orange and slice thinly. Place the orange slices in the base of a greased 1·1-litre (2-pint) pudding basin. Cream the margarine and sugar together and beat in the eggs, a little at a time. Fold in the flour and cocoa and enough milk to mix to a dropping consistency. Turn the mixture into the pudding basin, cover with greased greaseproof paper and foil and secure with string. Place in the electric casserole with boiling water to come halfway up the basin. Place the lid in position and cook on high for 3–4 hours.

Honey lemon surprise pudding

For the pastry
175 g (6 oz) self raising flour
pinch of salt
75 g (3 oz) shredded suet
water to mix

For the filling
100 g (4 oz) fresh white breadcrumbs
100 g (4 oz) soft brown sugar
60 ml (4 level tbsp) clear honey
1 large ripe lemon

To make the pastry: sift the flour and salt together into a mixing bowl. Stir in the suet and enough cold water to mix to a soft dough. Knead lightly. Roll out the dough and use two thirds to line a greased 900-ml (1½-pint) pudding basin.

To make the filling: stir the crumbs, brown sugar, honey and grated lemon rind together. Using a serrated knife cut away all the pith from the lemon, leaving it whole. Fill the basin with the crumb mixture pressing the whole lemon into the centre. Cover with the remaining pastry and seal the edges well. Cover with greased greaseproof paper and foil. Place in the electric casserole with boiling water to come halfway up the basin. Place the lid in position and cook on high for 4–5 hours.

Chocolate pear upsidedown cake

✦ Chocolate pear upsidedown cake

Pear halves and walnuts with light airy chocolate sponge underneath

For the topping
45 ml (3 level tbsp) brown sugar
15 g (½ oz) melted butter
439-g (15½-oz) can pear halves, drained
25 g (1 oz) walnuts, chopped

For the chocolate sponge
100 g (4 oz) soft tub margarine
100 g (4 oz) caster sugar
2 eggs, beaten
75 g (3 oz) self raising flour
25 g (1 oz) cocoa powder

To make the topping: grease a 20-cm (8-in) round cake tin and line it with greaseproof paper. Sprinkle the base of the tin with brown sugar and spoon over the melted butter. Fill the centre of each pear half with walnuts and place cut side down in the tin.

To make the sponge: cream the margarine and sugar together in a mixing bowl until pale and fluffy. Gradually beat in the eggs and fold in the flour and cocoa powder. Spoon the sponge mixture over the pears and smooth the top. Cover the tin with greased greaseproof paper and foil. Place the tin in the electric casserole with boiling water to come halfway up the tin. Place the lid in position and cook on high for 1½–2 hours. Turn out the cake and serve hot or cold with whipped cream.
Freeze without the walnuts

Old fashioned plum duff

You need to soak the currants and raisins in the sherry overnight before you start. When cooked, turn the plum duff out on to a heated plate and serve with cream or a sweet white sauce

175 g (6 oz) currants
50 g (2 oz) raisins
60 ml (4 tbsp) sherry
100 g (4 oz) self raising flour
5 ml (1 level tsp) ground cinnamon
5 ml (1 level tsp) ground mixed spice
100 g (4 oz) fresh white breadcrumbs
100 g (4 oz) shredded suet
75 g (3 oz) light soft brown sugar
1 egg, lightly beaten
60 ml (4 tbsp) milk

Soak the currants and raisins in the sherry overnight in a covered bowl. Sift the flour and spices into a large bowl and stir in the bread-crumbs, suet, sugar and fruit. Mix to a soft consistency with the egg and milk. Turn the mixture into a greased 1·1-litre (2-pint) pudding basin and cover with greased greaseproof paper and foil and secure with string. Place in the electric casserole with boiling water to come halfway up the side of the basin. Place the lid in position and cook on high for 3–4 hours.

Mincemeat ring

Serve with hot custard sauce

100 g (4 oz) self raising flour
1·25 ml (¼ level tsp) salt
50 g (2 oz) shredded suet
milk to mix
450 g (1 lb) mincemeat
sifted icing sugar

Stir the flour, salt and suet together in a bowl. Add enough milk to mix to a soft dough. Roll out on a floured surface to an oblong 20·5 × 30·5 cm (8 × 12 in). Spread the mincemeat over the surface of the pastry and roll up lengthways. Place in a greased 18-cm (7-in) ring mould and seal the edges well. Cover with greased greaseproof paper and foil and place in the electric casserole with boiling water to come halfway up the ring mould. Place the lid in position and cook on high for 3–4 hours. Remove from the ring mould and dust with icing sugar.

Pineapple canary pudding

For an Apricot canary pudding use the same size can of apricot halves instead of the pineapple

226-g (8-oz) can pineapple pieces
100 g (4 oz) soft tub margarine
100 g (4 oz) caster sugar
2 eggs, beaten
grated rind of 1 lemon
175 g (6 oz) self raising flour

For the glaze
25 g (1 oz) butter
30 ml (2 level tbsp) demerara sugar
15 ml (1 level tbsp) golden syrup

Drain the can of pineapple, reserve the juice

and chop the fruit. Cream together the margarine and sugar in a mixing bowl until light and fluffy. Beat in the eggs a little at a time. Fold in the pineapple pieces, lemon rind and flour. Turn the mixture into a greased 900-ml (1½-pint) pudding basin. Cover with greased greaseproof paper and foil and secure with string. Place in the electric casserole with boiling water to come halfway up the basin. Place the lid in position and cook on high for 3–4 hours.

To make the glaze: pour the pineapple juice into a small pan and boil until reduced to 15 ml (1 tbsp). Stir in the remaining ingredients and heat until the sugar has dissolved.

Bread and butter pudding

4 thin slices buttered bread
100 g (4 oz) mixed dried fruit
45 ml (3 level tbsp) demerara sugar
2 eggs
568 ml (1 pint) milk
5 ml (1 tsp) vanilla essence

Cut the bread slices in half and arrange in layers, buttered side up, in a greased 1·1–1·4-litre (2–2½-pint) pudding basin or soufflé dish. Sprinkle each layer with fruit and sugar. Lightly beat the eggs, milk and vanilla essence together. Pour over the pudding and leave to stand for 10 minutes then cover with foil and secure with string. Place in the electric casserole with boiling water to come halfway up the basin. Place the lid in position and cook on high for 3–4 hours.

Blackberry bread and butter pudding

4 thin slices buttered wholemeal bread
225 g (8 oz) fresh blackberries, picked over and washed
75 g (3 oz) demerara sugar
2 eggs
568 ml (1 pint) milk
2·5 ml (½ tsp) vanilla essence

Cut the bread slices in half and arrange in layers, buttered side up, in a greased 1·1–1·4-litre

(2–2½-pint) pudding basin or soufflé dish. Sprinkle each layer with fruit and sugar. Lightly beat the eggs, milk and vanilla essence together. Pour over the pudding and leave to stand for 10 minutes then cover with foil. Place in the electric casserole with boiling water to come halfway up the basin. Place the lid in position and cook on high for 3–4 hours.

Hot autumn pudding

A variation of the popular Summer pudding

6 slices white bread
225 g (8 oz) cooking apples, peeled, cored and sliced
225 g (8 oz) pears, peeled, cored and chopped
225 g (8 oz) red plums, halved and stoned
100 g (4 oz) fresh white breadcrumbs
100 g (4 oz) caster sugar
10 ml (2 level tsp) ground cinnamon

Arrange four slices of bread around the side and base of a greased 900-ml (1½-pint) pudding basin. Arrange the fruit and breadcrumbs in layers in the basin, sprinkling each fruit layer with sugar and cinnamon. Push well down and place the remaining two slices of bread on top. Cover with greased greaseproof paper and foil and secure with string. Place in the electric casserole with enough boiling water to come halfway up the basin. Place the lid in position and cook on high for 3–4 hours.

Apple Charlotte

For a crisp topping, place the apple Charlotte under a hot grill for 1–2 minutes until golden brown

900 g (2 lb) cooking apples
grated rind of 1 lemon
50 g (2 oz) demerara sugar
30 ml (2 level tbsp) apricot jam
caster sugar
225 g (8 oz) white breadcrumbs

Peel, core and slice the apples thinly. Place in a greased 900-ml (1½-pint) ovenproof dish with the lemon rind, demerara sugar and jam. Stir the caster sugar and breadcrumbs together and

spoon over the apples. Cover with greased greaseproof paper and foil. Place in the electric casserole with boiling water to come halfway up the dish. Place the lid in position and cook on high for 3–4 hours.

Orange fudge pudding

ILLUSTRATED IN COLOUR FACING PAGE 65

1 large orange, peeled and sliced into four rings
125 g (5 oz) butter
25 g (1 oz) light soft brown sugar
100 g (4 oz) caster sugar
2 eggs, beaten
100 g (4 oz) self raising flour
30–45 ml (2–3 tbsp) milk

Place the orange slices in the bottom of a greased 900-ml (1½-pint) pudding basin. Dot with 25 g (1 oz) butter and sprinkle with the soft brown sugar.

Beat the remaining butter and the caster sugar together in a mixing bowl until light and fluffy. Beat in the eggs and fold in the flour. Mix in the milk and spoon the sponge mixture on top of the oranges. Cover with a layer of greased greaseproof paper and foil. Place in the electric casserole with boiling water to come halfway up the basin. Place the lid in position and cook on high for 3–4 hours.

Spicy Dutch apple pudding

A delicious mixture of apples, dates and walnut with ginger

For the pastry
200 g (8 oz) self raising flour
1·25 ml (¼ level tsp) salt
100 g (4 oz) shredded suet

For the filling
800 g (1¾ lb) cooking apples, peeled, cored and sliced
30 ml (2 tbsp) lemon juice
100 g (4 oz) soft brown sugar
5 ml (1 level tsp) cornflour
10 ml (2 level tsp) ground ginger
50 g (2 oz) walnuts, chopped
100 g (4 oz) dates, chopped

To make the pastry: sift the flour and salt together into a mixing bowl. Stir in the suet and mix with cold water to a soft dough. Knead gently, roll out and use two thirds of the pastry to line a 1·4-litre (2½-pint) pudding basin.

To make the filling: place the apples, lemon juice and sugar in a saucepan and cook for 5 minutes until soft. Mix the cornflour to a smooth paste with a little water. Stir into the apple with the ginger and cook for 1–2 minutes, until the mixture thickens. Fill the pudding with layers of apple mixture, walnuts and dates. Cover with the remaining pastry and seal the edges. Cover with greased greaseproof paper and foil and secure with string. Place in the electric casserole with boiling water to come halfway up the basin. Place the lid in position and cook on high for 3–4 hours.

Blackberry and apple pudding

When cooked turn out and serve hot with custard sauce or cold with whipped cream

For the pastry
225 g (8 oz) self raising flour
pinch of salt
100 g (4 oz) shredded suet
cold water to mix

For the filling
275 g (10 oz) cooking apples, peeled
75 g (3 oz) demerara sugar
5 ml (1 level tsp) ground cinnamon
225 g (8 oz) blackberries, washed
15 ml (1 level tbsp) cornflour

To make the pastry: stir the flour, salt and suet together in a mixing bowl and add enough water to mix to a firm dough.

Core the apples and cut into rings. Place three large rings over the base of a greased 15-cm (6-in) round cake tin. Sprinkle with 30 ml (2 level tbsp) demerara sugar.

Use two thirds of the pastry to line the base and sides of the cake tin, placing it on top of the apple rings and sugar. Place the remaining apple in the pastry.

Wash and pick over the blackberries and add

the sugar, cinnamon and cornflour. Place the mixture in the pastry case. Cover the top with the remaining pastry and seal the edges. Cover the tin with greased greaseproof paper and foil. Place in the electric casserole with boiling water to come halfway up the tin. Place the lid in position and cook on high for 3–4 hours.

Christmas pudding

Store in the usual way and reheat when needed. Serve with brandy butter, cream or custard sauce. 5 ml (1 level tsp) mixed spice can be used instead of the mace, nutmeg and cinnamon

100 g (4 oz) fresh white breadcrumbs
100 g (4 oz) plain flour
1·25 ml (¼ level tsp) salt
1·25 ml (¼ level tsp) ground mace
1·25 ml (¼ level tsp) ground nutmeg
1·25 ml (¼ level tsp) ground cinnamon
100 g (4 oz) shredded suet
75 g (3 oz) caster sugar
75 g (3 oz) soft brown sugar
75 g (3 oz) mixed candied peel, finely chopped
100 g (4 oz) currants
75 g (3 oz) sultanas
200 g (7 oz) stoned raisins
50 g (2 oz) almonds, blanched and chopped
1 cooking apple, peeled, cored and chopped
grated rind and juice of ½ lemon
grated rind and juice of ½ orange
30 ml (2 tbsp) brandy
1 large egg, beaten
45–60 ml (3–4 tbsp) milk

Mix all the dry ingredients together and stir in the almonds, apple, orange and lemon rind. Mix the lemon and orange juice plus the brandy and eggs together and stir into the dry ingredients with enough milk to mix to a soft dropping consistency. Turn into a greased 900-ml (1½-pint) pudding basin and cover with greased greaseproof paper and foil. Place in the electric casserole with boiling water to come halfway up the basin. Place the lid in position and cook on high for 6–8 hours. Check the water after 3–4 hours' cooking. Replace the greaseproof paper and foil and store in a cool dry place until required.

Reheat on high for 2–3 hours before serving.

Plum upsidedown pudding

ILLUSTRATED IN COLOUR ON THE JACKET

When cooked turn the pudding out on to a heated plate and serve with Cornish ice cream

30 ml (2 level tbsp) redcurrant jelly
325 g (12 oz) red plums
25 g (1 oz) whole blanched almonds
100 g (4 oz) soft tub margarine
100 g (4 oz) caster sugar
2 eggs, beaten
100 g (4 oz) self raising flour
50 g (2 oz) ground almonds
2·5 ml (½ tsp) almond essence

Melt the redcurrant jelly in a saucepan and spoon half of it into a greased 18-cm (7-in) cake tin. Halve and stone the plums. Place each half cut side down in the base of the tin with a whole almond inside the stone cavity. Cream the margarine and sugar together in a mixing bowl until light and fluffy. Beat in the eggs and fold in the flour, ground almonds and essence. Turn the creamed mixture into the tin and smooth the surface. Cover with greased greaseproof paper and foil. Place in the electric casserole with boiling water to come halfway up the tin. Place the lid in position and cook on high for 1½–2 hours. Glaze with the rest of the redcurrant jelly before serving.

Stuffed cider-baked apples

4 large cooking apples
25 g (1 oz) butter
50 g (2 oz) soft brown sugar
2·5 ml (½ level tsp) ground cinnamon
50 g (2 oz) dates, chopped
25 g (1 oz) walnuts, chopped
300 ml (½ pint) cider
15 ml (1 level tbsp) cornflour

Wash and remove the cores from the apples. Slit the skin around the centre of each with a knife. Mix all the other ingredients together, except the cider and cornflour, in a small bowl. Spoon the filling into the centre of each apple. Place the apples in the electric casserole and pour the cider around them. Place the lid in position and cook on high for 3–4 hours or low for 6–8 hours.

Stuffed cider-baked apples

5 minutes before the end of cooking time, remove the apples from the electric casserole and place on a serving dish and keep warm. Mix the cornflour to a smooth paste with a little water and stir into the cider. Replace the lid and continue cooking. Pour over the apples and serve with whipped cream.

✣ Pineapple and apricot flambé

Serve with thick pouring cream and shortbread fingers

1 small fresh pineapple
4 oranges
325 g (12 oz) fresh apricots or 175 g (6 oz) dried
**   apricots**
60 ml (4 level tbsp) thick honey
2·5 ml (½ level tsp) ground cinnamon
50 g (2 oz) butter
150 ml (¼ pint) water
60 ml (4 tbsp) rum or vodka

Trim both the ends of the pineapple and cut into 1-cm (½-in) slices. Remove the skin with a sharp knife and the centre with an apple corer.

Cut each ring into six to eight segments. Peel the oranges, remove all the pith and cut into segments. Halve and stone the fresh apricots. Heat the honey, cinnamon, butter and water together and pour into the electric casserole with all the fruit. Place the lid in position and cook on high for 1–2 hours or low for 2–4 hours.

Just before serving remove the lid, pour over the rum or vodka, ignite and serve immediately.

Freeze without the rum or vodka

✤ Sherried apricot and raisin compote

225 g (8 oz) dried apricots
50 g (2 oz) seedless raisins
150 ml (¼ pint) water
30 ml (2 tbsp) sherry
grated rind and juice of 1 orange
grated rind and juice of 1 lemon
25 g (1 oz) sugar
15 g (½ oz) butter
5 ml (1 level tsp) ground cinnamon
15 ml (1 tbsp) brandy
60 ml (4 tbsp) double cream

Place all the ingredients, except the brandy and cream, in the electric casserole. Place the lid in position and cook on high for 2–3 hours or low for 4–6 hours. Heat the brandy in a spoon, ignite and pour over the apricots. Divide between serving dishes and top with cream.

Freeze without the cream

✤ Pear and macaroon dessert

Pear and raisins cooked in brandy and wine and topped with crushed macaroons and soured cream

6 fresh pears
75 g (3 oz) seedless raisins
50 g (2 oz) soft brown sugar
5 ml (1 level tsp) grated lemon rind
60 ml (4 tbsp) brandy
150 ml (¼ pint) sweet white wine
8 macaroons, crushed
142-ml (5-fl oz) carton soured cream

Peel and core the pears and cut into thin slices.

Stir the raisins, sugar and lemon rind together. Arrange the pears and raisin mixture in alternate layers in the electric casserole. Stir the brandy and wine together and pour over the fruit. Place the lid in position and cook on high for 1–2 hours or low for 2–4 hours. Spoon the fruit mixture into serving dishes and allow to cool. Sprinkle crushed macaroons over the top and serve the soured cream separately.

Freeze without the macaroons and soured cream

✤ Cranberries in port wine

25 g (1 oz) butter, melted
100 g (4 oz) sugar
grated rind and juice of ½ lemon
150 ml (¼ pint) port
450 g (1 lb) cooking apples, peeled, cored and sliced
450 g (1 lb) cranberries
142-ml (5-fl oz) carton double cream
50 g (2 oz) walnuts, chopped

Place all the ingredients except the cream and walnuts in the electric casserole. Place the lid in position and cook on high for 2–3 hours or low for 4–6 hours.

Turn into serving dishes. Whip the cream lightly until it holds its shape. Divide between the serving dishes and top with the chopped walnuts.

Freeze without the cream and walnuts

✤ Spiced orange rhubarb

Serve with cream or custard sauce or top with a crumble mixture

900 g (2 lb) rhubarb
100 g (4 oz) sugar
2·5 ml (½ level tsp) ground cinnamon
3 whole cloves
grated rind and juice of 1 orange
150 ml (¼ pint) water

Trim the rhubarb and cut it into 2·5-cm (1-in) pieces. Place in the electric casserole with the remaining ingredients. Place the lid in position and cook on high for 1–2 hours or low for 3–4 hours.

Baked apricot trifle

ILLUSTRATED IN COLOUR FACING PAGE 64

Serve this delicious trifle hot or well chilled

225-g (8-oz) jam Swiss roll
450 g (1 lb) fresh apricots, halved and stoned
60 ml (4 tbsp) brandy
2 eggs
2 egg yolks
568 ml (1 pint) creamy milk
45 ml (3 level tbsp) sugar
nutmeg
142-ml (5-fl oz) carton double cream
split toasted almonds

Cut the Swiss roll into twelve slices and use it to line the base and sides of a 1·1-litre (2-pint) ovenproof dish. Place the apricots in the dish, reserving one for decoration. Pour over the brandy and leave the mixture to soak for 10 minutes. Whisk the whole eggs and the extra yolks together. Heat the milk and sugar together until the sugar dissolves. Pour on to the eggs. Strain carefully into the dish to avoid disturbing the Swiss roll slices. Grate a little nutmeg over the top. Cover with greased greaseproof paper and foil. Place in the electric casserole with boiling water to come halfway up the dish. Place the lid in position and cook on high for 2–3 hours.

Just before serving whip the cream lightly, spoon over the trifle and sprinkle with almonds. When serving cold, use the reserved apricot to decorate the trifle.

Victoria plum meringue

The electric casserole cooks fruit so gently that it retains its shape and flavour

1 egg, separated
100 ml (4 fl oz) sweet sherry
about 15 boudoir biscuits
450 g (1 lb) Victoria plums
75 g (3 oz) caster sugar

Beat together the egg yolk and sherry. Dip the boudoir biscuits in the egg and sherry mixture and arrange round the sides of a 900-ml (1½-pint) ovenproof dish. Halve and stone the plums. Pile in the centre of the dish and sprinkle

half the sugar over them. Cover the dish with greased greaseproof paper and foil. Place in the electric casserole with boiling water to come halfway up the dish. Place the lid in position and cook on high for 1–2 hours or low for 2–4 hours.

Remove the greaseproof paper and foil. Whisk the egg whites until stiff, whisk in half the remaining sugar and fold in the rest. Pipe the meringue round the edge of the dish and cook under a medium grill for 1–2 minutes until golden brown.

✤ Hot plum and orange compote

Serve with soft sponge fingers

450 g (1 lb) red plums
25 g (1 oz) seedless raisins
100 ml (4 fl oz) medium dry sherry
45 ml (3 level tbsp) dark brown sugar
1 large orange
1 cinnamon stick
142-ml (5-fl oz) carton soured cream

Cut the plums in half and remove the stones. Place all the ingredients in the electric casserole and stir. Place the lid in position and cook on high for 1–2 hours or low for 2–4 hours. Serve the compôte hot with cream spooned over it.
Freeze without the cream

Cherry and walnut stuffed pears

Serve hot or well chilled with lightly whipped cream

4–6 medium-sized pears
50 g (2 oz) butter, softened
50 g (2 oz) soft brown sugar
50 g (2 oz) glacé cherries, chopped
50 g (2 oz) walnuts, chopped
15 ml (1 tbsp) Kirsch
50 g (2 oz) sugar
300 ml (½ pint) water

Peel the pears thinly. Remove the cores leaving the pears whole. Cream the butter and sugar together until light and fluffy. Stir in the cherries and nuts and fill the centre of each pear with the mixture. Place in the electric casserole. Stir the Kirsch, sugar and water together and pour over the pears. Place the lid in position and cook on high for 1–2 hours or low for 2–4 hours.

Creamed rice pudding

A quick to prepare, creamy rice pudding

100 g (4 oz) pudding rice
170-g (6-oz) can evaporated milk
300 ml (½ pint) milk
50 g (2 oz) caster sugar
ground nutmeg

Lightly grease the electric casserole. Add all the ingredients and stir well. Place the lid in position and cook on high for 1½–2 hours or low for 3–4 hours.

Poached mixed fruits

Dried fruit plumps up and cooks beautifully in the electric casserole – no need to soak it beforehand. Serve with cream or custard sauce

325 g (12 oz) dried mixed fruit, e.g.
apricots, prunes, apples, pears
400 ml (¾ pint) water
150 ml (¼ pint) sweet sherry
50 g (2 oz) sugar
1·25 ml (¼ level tsp) ground cinnamon

Place all the ingredients in the electric casserole and stir well. Place the lid in position and cook on high for 1–2 hours or low for 2–4 hours.

Baked egg custard

Baked egg custard made in the electric casserole is superb. Serve it hot or well chilled with stewed fruit

3 eggs
50–75 g (2–3 oz) sugar, to taste
568 ml (1 pint) milk
2·5 ml (½ tsp) vanilla essence
2·5 ml (½ level tsp) ground nutmeg

Place all the ingredients, except the nutmeg,

into a bowl and whisk together. Pour into a 900-ml (1½-pint) ovenproof dish and sprinkle with the nutmeg. Cover with greaseproof paper and foil and place in the electric casserole with boiling water to come halfway up the dish. Place the lid in position and cook on high for 3–4 hours or low for 6–7 hours.

Orange tapioca pudding

A variation is chocolate and orange tapioca: stir 50–75g (2–3 oz) plain chocolate into the tapioca with the orange segments.

568 ml (1 pint) creamy milk
50 g (2 oz) tapioca
30 ml (2 level tbsp) sugar
2 oranges

Heat the milk in a saucepan until almost boiling. Stir in the tapioca, sugar and finely grated rind of 1 orange. Brush the electric casserole with some melted butter and pour in the tapioca mixture. Place the lid in position and cook on high for 2–3 hours or low for 4–6 hours. Meanwhile remove the pith from the oranges and cut into segments.

30 minutes before the end of cooking time stir in the orange segments, replace the lid and continue cooking.

Sultana and semolina pudding

Spicy semolina pudding topped with meringue and grilled to a golden brown

568 ml (1 pint) milk
60 ml (4 level tbsp) semolina
5 ml (1 level tsp) mixed spice
grated rind of ½ lemon
50 g (2 oz) sultanas
2 eggs, separated
75 g (3 oz) sugar

Heat the milk, sprinkle on the semolina and cook for 2 minutes. Stir in the spice, lemon rind, sultanas, egg yolks and half the sugar. Pour into the electric casserole and place the lid in position. Cook on high for 1–2 hours or low for 2–4 hours.

Just before serving whisk the egg whites stiffly and fold in the remaining sugar. Spoon on top of the semolina and brown under a medium grill.

✤ Summer berries in wine

ILLUSTRATED IN COLOUR FACING PAGE 65

Serve hot or well chilled with shortbread fingers.

450 g (1 lb) mixed summer fruits, e.g. raspberries, blackcurrants, redcurrants, gooseberries
300 ml (½ pint) white wine
300 ml (½ pint) water
50 g (2 oz) sugar

Place all the ingredients in the electric casserole and stir well. Place the lid in position and cook on high for 1–2 hours or low for 2–4 hours.

Chocolate crumb pudding

Serve this delicious chocolate pudding with hot chocolate sauce

50 g (2 oz) chocolate
75 g (3 oz) butter or margarine
75 g (3 oz) caster sugar
1 egg, separated
2·5–5 ml (½–1 tsp) vanilla essence
100 g (4 oz) fresh white breadcrumbs
50 g (2 oz) self raising flour
60–75 ml (4–5 tbsp) milk

Melt the chocolate in a basin over hot water. Cream the fat and sugar together until pale and fluffy. Beat in the melted chocolate, egg yolk and vanilla essence. Stir the breadcrumbs and flour together and fold into the creamed mixture with enough milk to mix to a dropping consistency. Fold in the stiffly beaten egg white and turn into a greased 900-ml (1½-pint) pudding basin. Cover with greased greaseproof paper and secure with string. Place in the electric casserole with boiling water to come halfway up the side of the basin. Place the lid in position and cook on high for 3–4 hours.

Crème caramel

ILLUSTRATED IN COLOUR FACING PAGE 65

100 g (4 oz) granulated sugar
568 ml (1 pint) milk
284-ml (½-pint) carton single cream
3 eggs, beaten
40 g (1½ oz) caster sugar

Place the granulated sugar in a small pan with 150 ml (¼ pint) of water. Heat slowly until the sugar has dissolved, then bring to the boil and cook until golden brown. Pour the caramel into a greased 1·1-litre (2-pint) soufflé or ovenproof dish. Warm the milk and cream and pour on to the lightly whisked eggs and caster sugar. Strain the milk and egg mixture into the soufflé dish on top of the caramel. Cover with greased greaseproof paper and foil and place in the electric casserole with boiling water to come halfway up the dish. Place the lid in position and cook on high for 4–5 hours or low for 8–10 hours.

Remove the soufflé dish from the electric casserole and leave to cool before turning out.

Duchesse pudding

Serve this fruity pudding with a jam sauce

100 g (4 oz) butter or margarine
100 g (4 oz) caster sugar
2 eggs, beaten
30 ml (2 tbsp) seedless raisins
30 ml (2 tbsp) chopped glacé cherries
30 ml (2 tbsp) chopped mixed peel
30 ml (2 tbsp) chopped walnuts
few drops almond essence
175 g (6 oz) self raising flour
milk to mix

Cream the fat and sugar until pale and fluffy. Beat in the eggs, a little at a time. Stir in the fruit, nuts and almond essence. Fold in the flour and add a little milk to mix to a soft dropping consistency. Turn the mixture into a greased 900-ml (1½-pint) pudding basin. Cover with greased greaseproof paper and secure with string. Place in the electric casserole with boiling water to come halfway up the side of the basin. Place the lid in position and cook on high for 3–4 hours.

Date and banana pudding

100 g (4 oz) soft tub margarine
100 g (4 oz) soft brown sugar
2 eggs, beaten
100 g (4 oz) self raising flour
2·5 ml (½ level tsp) mixed spice
30 ml (2 level tbsp) clear honey
50 g (2 oz) dates, chopped
2 firm bananas, skinned and sliced

Cream the margarine and sugar together until pale and fluffy. Beat in the eggs, a little at a time. Fold in the flour and mixed spice.

Spoon half the honey into a greased 18-cm (7-in) cake tin and place the dates and bananas on top. Spoon the sponge mixture over and smooth the surface. Cover with greased greaseproof paper and foil. Place in the electric casserole with boiling water to come halfway up the side of the tin. Place the lid in position and cook on high for 1½–2 hours. Turn out on to a heated serving plate and spoon over the remaining honey.

Fruit castle puddings

75 g (3 oz) butter or margarine
75 g (3 oz) caster sugar
1 egg, beaten
75–100 g (3–4 oz) currants or sultanas
150 g (5 oz) self raising flour
2·5 ml (½ level tsp) mixed spice
milk to mix

Cream the fat and sugar together until pale and fluffy. Beat in the egg, a little at a time, and stir in the currants or sultanas. Fold in the flour with the mixed spice and mix to a soft dropping consistency with a little milk. Divide the mixture between eight greased dariole moulds. Cover each with greased greaseproof paper and secure with string. Place in the electric casserole with boiling water to come halfway up the sides of the moulds. Place the lid in position and cook on high for 2–3 hours. Serve with hot custard sauce.

Apricot and apple pudding

175 g (6 oz) dried apricots, soaked overnight
225 g (8 oz) self raising flour
pinch of salt
75 g (3 oz) shredded suet
150 ml (¼ pint) water
700 g (1½ lb) cooking apples, peeled, cored and sliced
90 ml (6 level tbsp) sugar

Sift the flour and salt together in a bowl and stir in the suet. Add the water and mix to a firm dough. Turn on to a lightly floured surface and knead gently. Use two-thirds of the pastry to line a greased 1·1-litre (2-pint) pudding basin. Arrange the drained apricots and prepared apples in alternate layers, sprinkling each layer with sugar. Top with the pastry lid and cover with greased greaseproof paper. Secure with string and place in the electric casserole with boiling water to come halfway up the side of the basin. Place the lid in position and cook on high for 3–4 hours.

Others from the pot

Three cheese fondue

All you need to serve this as a complete deliciously different meal are cubes of fresh bread for dipping into the hot fondue.

300 ml (½ pint) dry cider
30 ml (2 level tbsp) tomato chutney
50 g (2 oz) blue cheese, grated
225 g (8 oz) Cheddar cheese, grated
225 g (8 oz) Gouda cheese, grated
salt and freshly ground pepper
30 ml (2 level tbsp) flour

Place the cider and chutney in the electric casserole, place the lid in position and heat on high for 20 minutes. Add the blue cheese a little at a time and stir until melted. Mix the remaining cheeses, the seasoning and the flour together and add to the electric casserole, a little at a time, stirring after each addition to make sure the cheese has melted. Replace the lid and turn the electric casserole to low until you are ready to eat.

Fruit cheesecake

65 g (2½ oz) butter, softened
65 g (2½ oz) caster sugar
65 g (2½ oz) ground almonds
2 eggs, separated
grated rind and juice of 1 orange
grated rind of 1 lemon
50 g (2 oz) stoned raisins
225 g (8 oz) curd cheese
25 g (1 oz) plain flour
4 digestive biscuits, crushed
25 g (1 oz) butter, melted

Line the base of an 18-cm (7-in) flan tin with greased greaseproof paper. Cream the butter and sugar together until light and creamy. Beat in the almonds, egg yolks, orange rind and juice, lemon rind, raisins and curd cheese. Fold in the flour. Whisk the egg whites stiffly and fold into the mixture. Pour the mixture into the prepared tin and cover with greased greaseproof paper and foil. Place the tin in the electric casserole with enough water to come halfway up the tin. Place the lid in position and cook on high for 3–4 hours or low for 6–8 hours.

Cool the cheesecake in the tin. Stir the biscuit crumbs into the melted butter and spoon the mixture over the cheesecake. Press down and leave to set in a cool place for about 1 hour. Turn out the cheesecake and serve with cream.

Farmhouse cake

ILLUSTRATED IN COLOUR ON THE JACKET

225 g (8 oz) wholemeal flour
225 g (8 oz) plain flour
5 ml (1 level tsp) mixed spice
5 ml (1 level tsp) bicarbonate of soda
175 g (6 oz) butter or soft tub margarine
225 g (8 oz) caster sugar
100 g (4 oz) sultanas
100 g (4 oz) raisins, stoned
25 g (1 oz) mixed peel
1 egg, beaten
300 ml (½ pint) milk to mix
demerara sugar or 100 g (4 oz) almond paste

Stir the flours, spice and bicarbonate of soda together in a mixing bowl. Rub in the fat until

Farmhouse cake

the mixture resembles breadcrumbs. Stir in the sugar, fruit and peel and mix to a dropping consistency with the egg and milk. Spoon the mixture into a greased and lined 18-cm (7-in) round cake tin and level the top. Cover with 2 layers of greaseproof paper and a layer of foil. Place in the electric casserole with boiling water to come halfway up the tin. Place the lid in position and cook on high for 5 hours. Do not remove lid until the last hour. Turn out and cool.

To make the topping, either sprinkle with demerara sugar or cover with almond paste and cook under a hot grill until golden brown. If using almond paste, roll it out to a circle a little larger than the cake, brush the top of the cake with egg white and place the paste on top, cutting away any surplus. Using a small fluted cocktail cutter, cut shapes from the remaining paste to decorate the top of the cake. Brush the almond paste with egg white before grilling.

Jam making

Fruit cooked in the electric casserole for jam gives you the maximum flavour and extracts the pectin for a good set. Fruit also retains its shape

To make apple, apricot, blackcurrant, damson, plum, gooseberry, strawberry, raspberry or greengage jam

Add 450 g (1 lb) sugar and 150 ml (¼ pint) water to each 450 g (1 lb) prepared fruit

Place the fruit and water in the electric casserole. Place the lid in position and cook on low for 5–6 hours.

Turn the contents of the electric casserole into a large saucepan. Add the sugar and cook over a low heat until it dissolves, stirring continuously. Bring to the boil and boil rapidly until setting point is reached. Remove the pan from the heat.

To test whether setting point has been reached place a spoonful of jam on a cold saucer. Allow it to cool then push a finger across the top of the jam. If it is at setting point the surface will wrinkle. If the jam is not at setting point continue cooking for 5–10 minutes and test again.

Leave to cool for 10 minutes. Stir well, pot and cover in the usual way.

Tangy lemon curd

ILLUSTRATED IN COLOUR ON THE JACKET

4 thin-skinned lemons
100 g (4 oz) butter
450 g (1 lb) sugar
4 eggs, beaten

Finely grate the rind from the lemons. Melt the butter in a saucepan and add the lemon rind, juice and sugar. Heat gently until the sugar dissolves, stirring continuously. Cool the mixture for about 5 minutes and beat in the eggs. Strain the mixture into a 1·1-litre (2-pint) pudding basin and cover with foil. Place in the electric casserole with boiling water to come halfway up the basin. Place the lid in position and cook on low for 3–3 ½ hours.

The curd separates slightly during cooking so beat it lightly, while still warm, until smooth and creamy. Pour into glass jars and cover in the normal way.

MAKES ABOUT 700 G (1 ½ LB)

Seville orange marmalade

ILLUSTRATED IN COLOUR ON THE JACKET

Seville oranges are in season from December to February

900 g (2 lb) Seville oranges
juice of 2 small lemons
1·1 litres (2 pints) water
1·8 kg (4 lb) granulated sugar

Wash and halve the oranges. Squeeze the juice from them and place in the electric casserole with the lemon juice and water. Reserve any orange pips and pulp and tie in a muslin bag. Slice the orange peel thinly and add to the juice with the bag of pips. Place the lid in position and cook on high for 3–4 hours or low for 6–8 hours, until the peel is tender.

Remove the bag of pips, squeeze out any juice and discard. Pour the contents of the electric casserole into a large saucepan. Add the sugar and cook over a gentle heat until the sugar dissolves. Bring to the boil and boil rapidly until setting point is reached (see jam making on page 93). Remove from the heat and leave to stand for 10 minutes. Stir well, then pot and cover in the usual way.

MAKES ABOUT 2·6 KG (6 LB)

Rum punch

900 ml (1½ pints) cold water
225 g (8 oz) sugar
1 lemon
2 oranges
150 ml (¼ pint) strong tea
150 ml (¼ pint) rum

Pour the water and sugar into the electric casserole. Peel the rind from the lemon and from one orange. Squeeze the juice from the lemon and oranges and add to the electric casserole with the remaining ingredients. Place

the lid in position and heat on high for 1 hour. Turn the casserole to low to keep the punch hot.

MAKES ABOUT 1·4 LITRES (2½ PINTS)

Mulled spiced wine

Brighten up a dull winter evening with this hot wine cup

1 bottle red wine
12 lumps of sugar
6 cloves
600 ml (1 pint) boiling water
150 ml (¼ pint) curaçao
150 ml (¼ pint) brandy, optional
grated nutmeg

Pour all the ingredients into the electric casserole, place the lid in position and heat on high for 1 hour. Turn the casserole to low to keep the wine hot.

MAKES 1·7 LITRES (3 PINTS)

Apple and tomato chutney

450 g (1 lb) apples, peeled and cored
450 g (1 lb) tomatoes, skinned
225 g (8 oz) onions, skinned
1 clove of garlic, skinned
100 g (4 oz) dried fruit
175 g (6 oz) demerara sugar
10 ml (2 level tsp) mustard seeds
10 ml (2 level tsp) curry powder
2·5 ml (½ level tsp) cayenne pepper
10 ml (2 level tsp) salt
400 ml (¾ pint) malt vinegar

Chop the apples, tomatoes, onions and garlic and place them in the electric casserole with the dried fruit and sugar. Tie the mustard seeds in a muslin bag and add to the electric casserole with the curry powder, cayenne pepper, salt and vinegar. Place the lid in position and cook on high for 3–4 hours or low for 6–8 hours. Remove the bag of mustard seeds and pot and cover in the usual way.

MAKES ABOUT 2 KG (4 LB)

Index